The Roman Gods
An Illustrated Introduction
Matthew Leigh Embleton

Copyright ©2024 Matthew Leigh Embleton. All rights reserved.

The Roman Gods

The Primordials 1
The Titans 3
The Olympians 5
Aion (Time, Ages, and Cycles of Time) 7
Apollo (The Renaissance Man of the Gods) 8
Aurora, Mater Matuta (The Dawn) 9
Bacchus, Fufluns (Wine, Fertility, and Festivity) 10
Bellona (War) 11
Bona Dea (The Good Goddess) 12
Caelus (The Sky) 13
Carmenta (Childbirth and Prophecy) 14
Ceres (Agriculture, Fertility, and the Harvest) 15
Concordia (Harmony and Concord) 16
Cupid, Amor (Love and Desire) 17
Diana (The Chaste Huntress and Protector) 18
Dies (The Day) 19
Discordia (Strife and Discord) 20
Egeria (Water Nymph of Laws and Rituals) 21
Empanda (Sanctuary and Protection) 22
Epona (Protector of Horses) 23
Falacer (Ancient God of the Sky) 24
Fatum (Impending Doom) 25
Faunus (The Wild Forests) 26
Februus (Purification, and the Underworld) 27
Feronia (The Wilderness, Fertility, and Abundance) 28
Fides (Trust, Faith, and Credibility) 29
Flora (Spring, Flowers, and New Growth) 30
Fontus (Wells and Springs) 31
Fortuna (Fortune and Luck) 32
Furrina (Springs and Runnning Water) 33
Genius (Spirit of Divine Nature) 34
The Gratiae (The Graces) 35
Hermaphroditus (The Ancient Androgynous One) 36
Honos (Honour, Valour, and Bravery) 37
Invidia, Invidentia (Divine Retributive Justice) 38
Iris (The Rainbow Messenger) 39
Janus (Beginnings, Openings, and Transitions) 40
Juno (Queen of the Gods) 41
Jupiter (King of the Gods) 42
Justitia (Divine Order, Justice, and Custom) 43
Juturna (Fountains, Wells, and Springs) 44
Juventas (Eternal Youth, and Forgiveness) 45
Latona (Motherhood, Protector of Children) 46
Lucifer (The Morning Star, The Light-Bringer) 47
Luna (The Moon) 48
Magna Mater (Great Mother of the Mountains) 49
Mare (The Primordial Sea) 50
Mars (War, Courage, Bravery, and Destruction) 51
Mercury (The Divine Messenger) 52
Minerva (Wisdom, Strategy, Battle, and Crafts) 53

Mithras (The Persian, Light, Truth, and Oaths) 54
Moneta (Memory and Remembrance) 55
Morpheus (The Shaper of Dreams) 56
Mors (Peaceful Death) 57
Natura (Nature) 58
Necessitas (Necessity, Compulsion, Inevitability) 59
Neptune (The Sea) 60
Nox (The Night) 61
Ops (Queen of the Heavens) 62
The Parcae (The Three Fates) 63
Pax (Peace) 64
Pluto, Orcus, and Dis Pater (The Underworld) 65
Pomona (Abundance, Fruit Trees) 66
Proserpina (The Underworld and Spring Growth) 67
Protogonus (The Creator) 68
Querella (Mockery, Satire, and Criticism) 69
Roma (The Roman State) 70
Salacia (The Depths of the Ocean) 71
Salus (Health, Healing, and Hygiene) 72
Saturn (Time and the Harvest) 73
Scotus (The Darkness) 74
Sol (The Sun) 75
The Somnia (The Dream Spirits) 76
Somnus (Sleep) 77
Spes (Hope) 78
Summamus (Nocturnal Thunder) 79
The Tenebrae (The Spirits of Death) 80
Terra Mater, Tellus Mater (Mother Earth) 81
Trivia (Magic, Spells, the Moon, and Crossroads) 82
Vejovis (Health, Healing, and Medicine) 83
The Venti (The Winds) 84
Venus (Love, Lust, Passion, and Procreation) 86
Veritas (Truth) 87
Vertumnus (The Change of Seasons) 88
Vesta (The Sacred Fire) 89
Victoria (Victory) 90
Virtus (Bravery and Virtue) 91
Volturnus (The Rivers) 92
Vulcan (Blacksmith of the Gods) 93

Cover: A Temple of Apollo
Source: AI Generated by the author

Acknowledgments

I have long been fascinated by languages and history, and I am very grateful to the special people in my life who have supported and encouraged me in my work. Thank you for believing in me. You know who you are.

Thanks to Jacobus Price for the AI image of Janus

Introduction

Who are the Roman gods?

The Roman gods are the key players in Roman mythology, an ancient collection of narratives that evolved over thousands of years to explain the origins of the forces of nature around us, their impact on our lives, the nature of humankind itself, what it means to be human, our relationship with the earth and the cosmos, and our sense of place within it.

How many gods are there in Roman mythology?

If we include all of the major gods, minor gods, spirits, demi-gods, mythical creatures, etc. from all of the different traditions across the ancient Roman world, we would be looking at about five hundred, and if all of them were included in this book, holding it and leafing through it would be a Herculean task, so this is an illustrated introduction to over eighty of them.

Why are there so many gods?

In all the corners of the ancient Roman world, there were local gods that protected and assisted people in many different aspects of their lives. Major gods even had local nicknames or epithets to emphasise the different characteristics that people resonated with. Romans who travelled far and wide through migration and trade learned of gods in other regions and brought them home with them, for example the Phrygian goddess Cybele (Magna Mater) in Anatolia, Asia Minor (modern day Turkey). Those with particular cunning would pray to the gods of their enemies to gain any advantage they could.

How do we know about these gods?

They are part of the history of Western literature from antiquity to the modern day, and from the Renaissance period and the revival of a classical education, they have inspired generations of storytellers, artists, authors, poets, and composers alike ever since.

Virgil's Aeneid

Virgil's Aeneid is an epic Latin poem that tells the legendary story of Aeneas, a Trojan who fled the fall of Troy and travelled to Italy, where be became the ancestor of the Romans. Written between 29 BCE and 19 BCE, the first half tells the story of Aeneas's wanderings from Troy to Italy, and the second half tells of the Trojans victorious war against the Latins. Figures from Roman mythology appear throughout, observing and influencing events.

Ovid's Metamorphoses

Ovid's Metamorphoses (from ancient Greek: μεταμόρφωσις, metamórphōsis (μετά, metá = change + μορφή, morphe = form) is a Latin narrative poem first published in 8 CE. The poem chronicles the history of the world from its creation to the deification of Julius Caesar in a mythical-historical framework of 250 myths, 15 books, and 11,995 lines.

Why are there so many different versions of the same stories?

There were hundreds of years of oral tradition and storytelling all over the Roman world before the events and relationships between the gods started to be written down. There were always multiple versions of the myths steadily evolving, depending on where you were, and who was telling the tale. It was the author's choice which versions they used, and they could distinguish themselves by using the well known source material to tell their version, embellishing here, making a few changes there, putting their own stamp on it, hopefully saying something new and interesting or adding a deeper meaning somewhere.

If we only look at one source, we miss out. For example, it is not until Ovid's Metamorphoses that we hear of Morpheus (one of my favourites) being named as the leader of the Oneiroi (the dream spirits). Other writers down the ages such as Aeschylus, Publius Vergilius Maro, Gaius Julius Hyginus, and Nonnus of Panopolis all added their contribution to the tradition. In the 10th century the Byzantine encyclopaedia of the ancient Mediterranean world known as the Suda (or Souda) collected and preserved many ancient sources that have since been lost.

It's all quite complicated isnt it?

Tell me about it... But that's also what makes it so fascinating. It's such a broad and multi-layered subject. No one will ever have the last word on it. For every person who tells a story, there will be another person who knows an additional detail, twist, or version of it.

Do people still believe in these gods?

People absolutely still choose to believe in the Roman gods in many different ways, and for many different reasons, i.e. paganism, astrology, etc., as they symbolise and represent so many aspects of who we are: our aspirations and failings, strengths and weaknesses, and hopes and dreams.

Interpretatio Graeca

The Romans studied Greek culture and adopted aspects of it to enhance their own culture, including among other things, their religion, gods, and mythology.

Where the Romans had no equivalent god, they adopted the Greek one. Where they found similarities between their gods and the Greek ones, it simply confirmed their beliefs and increased their sense of conviction that such a god did indeed exist, since it was worshipped in other traditions as well, just with a different name. This process is known as *Interpretatio Graeca* (interpretation by Greek models).

This is part of what made the Romans successful, when they were culturally outward-looking, when they didn't care where the ideas came from, if they were good ideas, then they would take the best of them and make them their own.

Family Trees of Gods

In the following pages, there are three family trees of gods: The Primordials, The Titans, and The Olympians. These family trees are roughly based on the Greek tradition, with the Greek names changed to their Roman counterparts where applicable.

The Roman Gods — *An Illustrated Introduction*

The Primordials

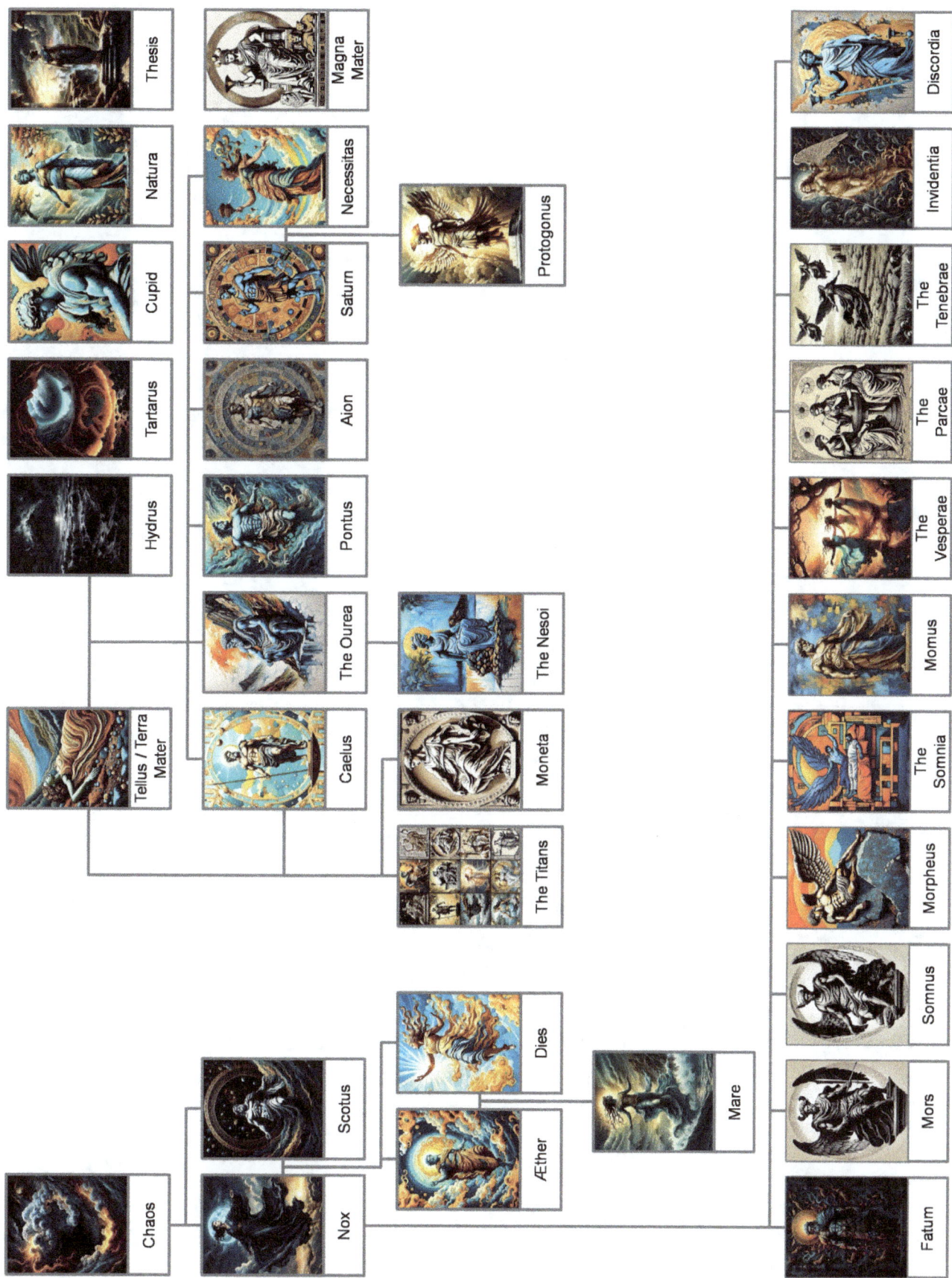

The Roman Gods *An Illustrated Introduction*

The Titans

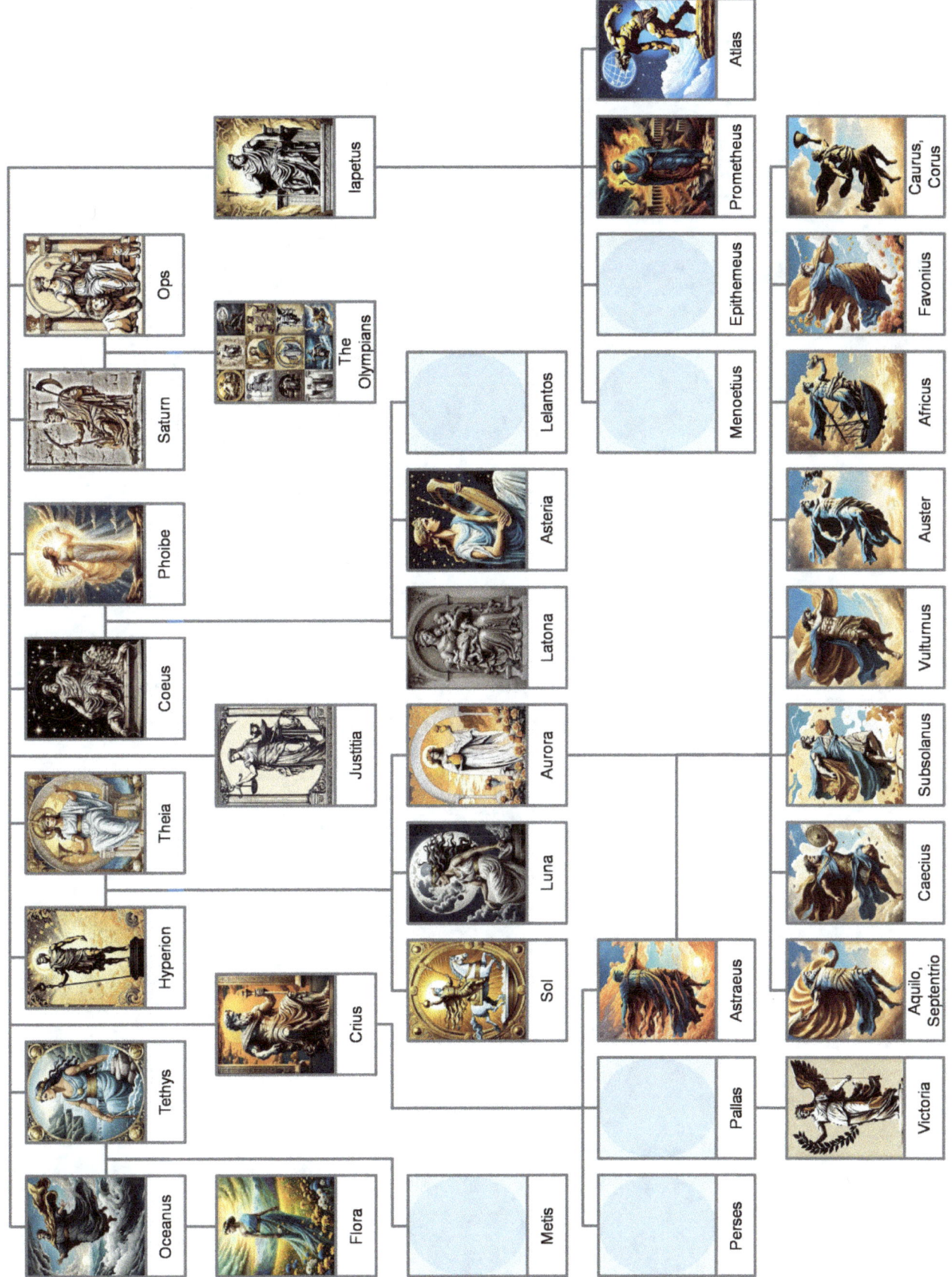

The Olympians

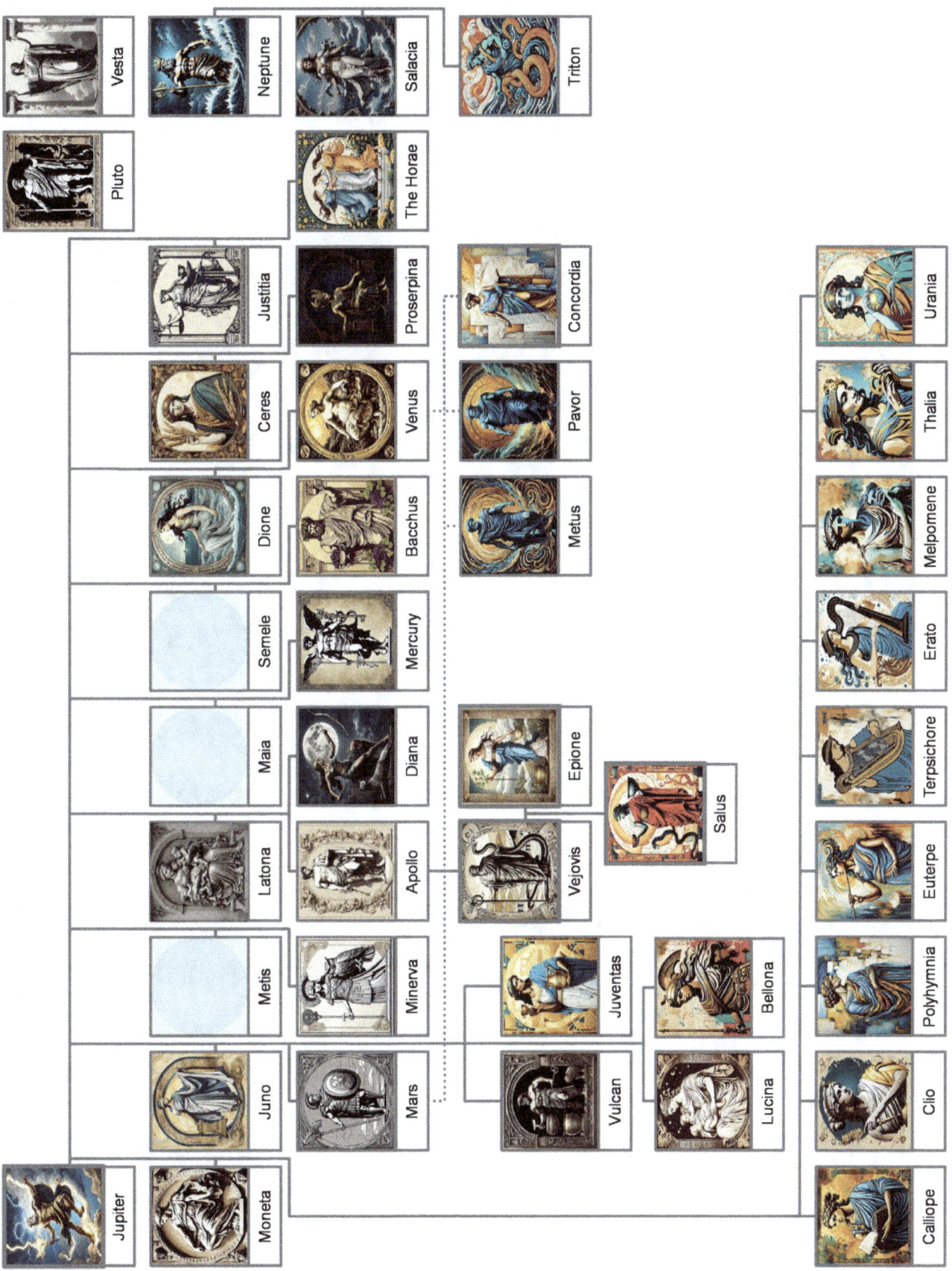

Aion (Time, Ages, and Cycles of Time)

Roman Name(s): Aion
Greek Name(s): *Aiών*, Aeon, Aion

Aion is a god of time in its various forms, including different ages, cycles of time (such as the year and the zodiac), perpetuity, and eternity. The English word aeon, which refers to a very long period of time, originates from this concept of Aion.

Because of Aion's association with time, he was identified and conflated with the Greek gods Chronos and Cronus, who in turn were identified and conflated with the Roman god Saturn as a Father Time figure, particularly in art from the Renaissance period onwards.

Aion is often depicted as a man (sometimes young, sometimes old) standing inside and turning a zodiac wheel decorated with zodiac signs representing the shifting constellations of stars and the cycles of time.

Another symbol that represents Aion is an Ouroboros, a serpent biting or swallowing its tail or hiding its tail underneath its body.

As a god of cyclic ages, Aion appears as an icon in several of the mystery religions where the concepts of eternity and the afterlife appear, such as the Mysteries of Cybele (Magna Mater), the Mysteries of Dionysus (Bacchus), Orphic Religion, and the Mysteries of Mithras.

In the Mysteries of Mithras, there also appears a lion-headed figure called a Leontocephalus (a lion-headed god), which is largely agreed by scholars to be a representation of time and seasonal change, and believed by some to be a version of Aion.

Perhaps the most well known depictions of Aion are the Roman mosaic at Sentium (modern-day Sassoferrato, central-eastern Italy), and the Roman mosaic at Hippo Regius (modern day Annaba, Algeria). Aion also appears on the silver Parabiago plate, found near Milan in 1907, depicted holding a sceptre and standing among a vast cosmic setting including the sun, the moon, the earth, the sea, and the seasons. It has been stylistically and technically dated to somewhere between the 2nd and 5th centuries CE.

Aion also became a symbol and a guarantor of the perpetuity of Roman rule, appearing on coins issued by emperor Antoninus Pius, the fourth of the so-called Five Good Emperors who reigned between 138 and 161 CE.

In the Roman tradition, Aion's female counterpart is Aeternitas (Eternity) or Anna Perenna (Perpetual Years), celebrated on the Ides of March (March 15th) in the old Roman Lunar Calendar when the year started in March.

Apollo (The Renaissance Man of the Gods)

Roman Name(s): Apollo
Greek Name(s): *Απολλων*, Apollôn, Apollo
Etruscan Name(s): Apulu

Apollo is the god of archery, hunting, protection, healing, prophecy, light, truth, and the arts.

He is the personification of multiple ideals of masculinity and youthful masculine beauty, and something of a Renaissance Man among the gods. The term Renaissance Man is used here with irony because:

1 - It refers to someone who is skilled in many disciplines in contrasting and complimentary fields (e.g. the sciences, the classics, and the arts).

2 - The Renaissance (rebirth) period of 15th century Europe saw a massive resurgence from east to west of classical culture, including preserved texts by Greek and Latin writers on the sciences, the arts, and classical mythology.

Apollo symbolises and embodies many qualities that were part of how the Romans saw themselves and what they aspired to, and perhaps this is why he is one of the more complex gods.

Apollo and his twin sister Diana (born to Jupiter and Latona) both symbolise archery, hunting, and the protection of the young. Apollo is credited with having invented archery, and such an invention is symbolic of brains over brawn or intelligence over brute force.

Like several of the Roman and Greek gods, Apollo was also known to the neighbouring Etruscans. In the late 6th century BCE a temple was built for the worship of *Aplu* (Apollo) in the ancient Etruscan city of Veii, on the southern limits of Etruria, approximately 10 miles north-northwest of Rome. Other temples also appeared in Falerii Veteres (Etruria), Pompeii, Rome, and Melite (Malta).

Medicine and healing are associated with Apollo partly by association with his son Vejovis (Asclepius). Apollo has the power to deliver people from epidemics, but also the power to bring ill health and deadly plague with his arrows.

Apollo is also associated with prophecy and foresightedness. The oracles in the temples of Apollo were often consulted for guidance. He also symbolises the giving or bringing of light, the light of the sun, the light of truth and reason, and warding off the darkness of evil.

He presides over the arts, music, songs, dance, and poetry. Another astrological symbol for Apollo incorporates the outline of a lyre.

Apollo is one of the *Dii Selecti* (the chosen gods), a list of the twenty principal gods of Roman religion according to Marcus Terentius Varro (recorded by Augustine of Hippo in his work *De Civitate Dei* or The City of God in the 5th century CE).

Aurora, Mater Matuta (The Dawn)

Roman Name(s): Aurora, Mater Matuta
Greek Name(s): *Hως, Êôs, Eos*
Etruscan Name(s): Thesan

Aurora is the goddess of the dawn who renews herself each morning and flies across the sky.

Her journey announces the arrival of her brother Sol (The Sun) and the beginning of the day.

She is also the sister of Luna (The Moon).

Roman writers avoided imitating the Greeks Hesiod and Homer with regard to her parentage.

According to Ovid, Aurora was also known as Pallantis or Pallantias, the daughter of Pallas (rather than the daughter of Hyperion).

Aurora and Astraeus together produced the Venti (The Winds). The first four of the Venti to be named were Aquilo (The North Wind), Subsolanus (The East Wind), Auster (The South Wind), and Favonius (The West Wind).

A goddess personifying something as fundamental and elemental to human daily life as the dawn can be traced back to the reconstructed Proto-Indo European name *Hausos* as far back as c. 4500 BCE.

The name Aurora contains traces of the name Hausos, along with the Vedic *Ushas*, Lithuanian *Aušrinė*, Latvian *Auseklis*, and the Germanic *Ēastre*.

Aurora was originally known as Mater Matuta, native to the ancient region of Latium, originally populated by the tribe known as the Latins or the Latians, where the name of the Latin language comes from, the region in which the city of Rome was founded.

Mater Matuta was originally thought of as a goddess of female fertility, childbirth, and the fertilisation and ripening of grain, but over time she became associated with the dawn.

Before the Roman Empire, before the Roman Republic, there was the Kingdom of Rome. The sixth king of Rome, Servius Tullius, was thought to have personally consecrated the temple of Mater Matuta some time between 578 BCE and 535 BCE.

Another temple for the worship of Mater Matuta was built in the ancient Etruscan port of Pyrgi. Because of its port location it has been suggested that she was also associated with ports and the sea.

The festival of Mater Matuta was known as Matralia and was celebrated on the 11th day of June.

Bacchus, Fufluns (Wine, Fertility, and Festivity)

Roman Name(s): Bacchus, Liber
Greek Name(s): Διονυσος, Dionysos, Dionysus
Etruscan Name(s): Fufluns

Bacchus is the god of wine making, orchards, fruit, vegetation, fertility, festivity, insanity, ritual madness, religious ecstasy, and the theatre.

The Greeks knew him as Dionysus, while the Etruscans knew him as Fufluns, perhaps as a god native to Fufluna in Etruria.

He is commonly depicted holding grapes and bearing a wine cup.

The astrological symbols for both Bacchus and Dionysus represent bunches of grapes.

Bacchus is also sometimes depicted holding a wand or staff of giant fennel, covered with ivy vines and leaves, sometimes topped with a pine cone, an artichoke, or fennel, a symbol of prosperity, fertility, and hedonism.

This wand of Bacchus is benificient, but it can also be used as a weapon against those who oppose his cult and the freedoms that he represents.

Those who partake in the rites and rituals of Bacchus are believed to become possessed and empowered by the god himself.

The name Bacchus (Bacchos, Βάκχος) is actually Greek in origin, meaning the frenzy that Bacchus is said to induce, known as *baccheia*. He was also identified with the earlier god Liber or Liber Pater (the free father).

The wine, music, and ecstatic dance of Bacchus freed his followers from self-conscious fear and care. Wine was a religious focus, and could ease suffering, bring joy, and inspire divine madness.

Festivals of Bacchus included the performance of sacred dramas and enactments of his myths, which is believed to be behind the development of the tradition of western theatre, hence his association with the theatre.

His father is Jupiter, but there are different accounts of who his mother is. Hesiod suggests Semele, Marcus Tullius Cicero suggests Selene (Luna) or her forerunner Bendis, and others suggest Dione.

Bacchus was celebrated during the Roman festival of Liberalia, but the Roman state viewed the festival of Bacchanalia as subversive, because of the free mixing of classes and the transgressions of social and moral constraints, so much so that its celebration was made a capital offence, except for the state sponsored toned-down versions.

The Roman Gods   An Illustrated Introduction

Bellona (War)

Roman Name(s): Bellona, Bella
Greek Name(s): *Ενυο, Ενυω*, Enyô, Enyo
Etruscan Name(s): Enie

Bellona is the goddess of war and bloodlust. She is commonly depicted wearing a military helmet, holding a sword, a spear, a shield, a torch, or a whip as she rides into battle on a four horse chariot. She is the female counterpart and close companion of the god Mars. Her name literally means war or warfare.

She was originally worshipped by the Sabine peoples in the central Apennine Mountains and around the ancient region of Latium before becoming assimilated into the Roman Republic, replacing an earlier ancient war goddess known as Nerio or Neriene, a wife of Mars to whom the spoils of war were dedicated. Aulus Gellius in his book *Attic Nights* states that the name Nerio is also of Sabine origin meaning strength and fortitude.

Bellona was also closely identified with Discordia, the goddess of strife. Homer identifies them by their Greek names (Enyo and Eris, respectively) as being the same goddess. She is said to delight in bloodshed and the destruction of towns. The temple of Bellona was dedicated to her in 296 BCE during the third of the Samnite Wars, a struggle for control of central and southern Italy in which the Romans were victorious.

On the 24th day of March, priests known as Bellonarii would wound their own arms or legs to offer her a blood sacrifice, a day which would be known as the day of blood (*dies sanguinis*). A festival to celebrate her and give thanks for success in war was celebrated separately on the 3rd day of June.

Bona Dea (The Good Goddess)

Roman Name(s): Bona Dea

Bona Dea (The Good Goddess) is the descriptive name of a secret goddess associated with chastity, fertility, married Roman women, healing, and the protection of the state and people of Rome. She is an example of the gods and goddesses who were worshipped at an official state level as well as personally and privately.

She is commonly depicted holding a cornucopia (a horn of plenty), with a snake or snakes (a powerful symbol of healing and medicine in the ancient world).

The cult of Bona Dea was introduced to Rome after 272 BCE from the coastal areas of Southern Italy (*Magna Graeca*) populated by Greek settlers from the 8th century BCE onwards.

The Temple of Bona Dea was built some time in the 3rd century BCE on the Aventine Hill of Ancient Rome. It was a centre of healing and a place where medicinal herbs were sold.

Men were barred from some of her rituals and gatherings, and only those who had been initiated into her tradition were given her true name. Her rites allowed the use of strong wine and blood-sacrifice, which were otherwise forbidden to them in the Roman tradition.

Male writers speculated about her true identity, believing her to be an aspect of Terra Mater, Ops, Cybele, Ceres, or Fauna who could prophesy the fates of women.

Bona Dea's cults in the city of Rome were led by priestesses of Vesta, another Roman goddess associated with chastity.

Caelus (The Sky)

Roman Name(s): Caelus
Greek Name(s): *Ουρανος*, Ouranos, Uranus

Caelus is a primordial god of the sky. His name literally means the sky or the heavens, which is where the English word celestial comes from.

Caelus has also been associated with Summamus, the ancient Roman god of nocturnal thunder, in contrast to Jupiter who was the god of thunder during the day.

This idea continued with Caelus being given the epithet Nocturnus (the night). Hence *Caelus Nocturnus* was the god of the night sky.

According to Cicero and Hyginus, Caelus was the son of Aether (The Daylight) and Dies (The Day).

In this version of the tradition, Caelus fathered Mercury with the goddess Dies, and fathered Janus with the goddess Trivia.

The Roman architect and engineer Vitruvius includes Caelus in a list of gods whose temple buildings should be built open to the sky.

As a god of the sky, Caelus became identified with Jupiter. In Volume VI of the Corpus Inscriptionum Latinarum (CIL 6.81.2), an inscription reads: "Optimus Maximus Caelus Aeternus Iup<pi>ter" (the best and greatest eternally heavenly Jupiter).

Carmenta (Childbirth and Prophecy)

Roman Name(s): Carmenta, Carmentis
Greek Name(s): *Νικοστράτη*, Nicostrate

Carmenta or Carmentis is a goddess of childbirth and prophecy, a protector of mothers and children, and a patron of midwives. She is associated with technological innovation, and she was also said to have invented the Latin alphabet.

She was originally of Greek origin. Her name in ancient Greek was Nicostrate (Νικο = victory + στράτη = army), and she came from Arcadia in the Peloponnese.

When her worship spread to the Italian peninsula, her name changed to Carmenta in order to honour her power of prophecy and predicting the future in her songs.

The name Carmenta comes from the Latin *carmen*, meaning a song, a poem, a magic spell, or an oracle. It is also where the English word charm comes from.

Hyginus in his Fabulae (no. 277) states that when Carmenta arrived in Italy, she had brought the Greek alphabet with her, but replaced fifteen of the letters in order to make the Latin alphabet.

A festival in her honour, Carmentalia, was celebrated from the 11th to the 15th of January, and it was forbidden to wear animal skin of any form in her temple.

Carmentis is one of the minor *Dii Flaminales*, gods who were cultivated by flamines, special priests who were assigned to the official cults during the Roman Republic.

Ceres (Agriculture, Fertility, and the Harvest)

Roman Name(s): Ceres
Greek Name(s): Δημητηρ, Dêmêtêr, Demeter
Etruscan Name(s): Zerene

Ceres is the goddess of agriculture, fertility, grains, the harvest, the earth, cultivated crops, sacred law, and the cycle of life and death.

Her name is where the English word cereal comes from.

The Greeks knew her as Demeter, and the Etruscans knew her as Zerene.

The astrological symbols for Ceres or Demeter represent a sickle.

She is credited with the discovery of spelt wheat, the yoking of oxen, the ploughing, sowing, protection and nourishment of young seed, and the gift of agriculture, sustaining humankind with the earth's rich bounty. Before this gift of agriculture, it was believed that humankind subsisted on acorns, wandering without settlement or laws.

Ceres has the power to fertilise, multiply, and fructify plant and animal seed, and her laws and rites protect all the activities of the agricultural cycle.

With her daughter Proserpina she was central to the Eleusinian Mysteries, a religious tradition that predated the Olympian pantheon, which may have had its roots in the Mycenaean period (c1400-1200 BCE). Initiates into the cult were promised a path to a blessed afterlife in the realm of Elysium.

The festival Cerealia was held in her honour from mid to late April, opening with a horse race in the Circus Maximus, whose starting point was opposite the Aventine Temple. Demeter (Ceres) is assigned the zodiac constellation Virgo (The Virgin) by Marcus Manilius in his 1st century work *Astronomicon*. In art, the constellation Virgo holds Spica, a sheaf of wheat in her hand.

Among Ceres's helper gods were • *Vervactor*, He who ploughs • *Reparātor*, He who prepares the earth • *Imporcĭtor*, He who ploughs with a wide furrow • *Insitor*, He who plants seeds • *Obarātor*, He who traces the first ploughing • *Occātor*, He who harrows • *Serritor*, He who digs • *Subruncinator*, He who weeds • *Mĕssor*, He who reaps • *Convector*, He who carries the grain • *Conditor*, He who stores the grain • *Promitor*, He who distributes the grain.

Ceres is one of the *Dii Selecti* (the chosen gods), a list of the twenty principal gods of Roman religion according to Varro (recorded by Augustine of Hippo in his work De Civitate Dei or The City of God in the 5th century CE).

Ceres is one of the minor *Dii Flaminales*, gods who were cultivated by flamines, special priests who were assigned to the official cults during the Roman Republic.

Concordia (Harmony and Concord)

Roman Name(s): Concordia
Greek Name(s): Ἁρμονια, Harmonia

Concordia is the goddess of concord and harmony. Concordia presides over marital harmony, soothing strife and discord. This later expanded to represent a more abstract sense of harmony, as a goddess who presides over the greater cosmic balance (depicted above allegorically balancing on one foot). Her opposite is the goddess Discordia (Eris).

She is the offspring of an adulterous affair between Venus (the goddess of Love) and Mars (the god of War). Venus's husband Vulcan punished Venus and Mars by catching them in a net, which he then showed to all the gods to ridicule.

Diodorus Siculus (5.8.42) alternatively suggests that Concordia was born of Jupiter (Zeus) and Electra, the Pleiad star nymph of Mount Saon on the island of Samothrace in the north Aegean Sea.

Concordia was awarded to Cadmus, the hero and founder of the city of Thebes, in a wedding attended by the gods. Vulcan never forgave Venus for her betrayal, and presented Concordia with a cursed necklace, which doomed her descendants to endless tragedy.

After a string of catastrophes the couple emigrated to Illyria where they battled various local tribes to form a new kingdom. They were later transformed into serpents by the gods and carried off to the Islands of the Blessed in Elysium to live in peace.

Cupid, Amor (Love and Desire)

Roman Name(s): Cupidus, Cupid, Amor
Greek Name(s): *Ερος*, Eros, Eros
Etruscan Name(s): Erus

Cupid is the god of love, desire, attraction, and affection. He is also known as Amor, the Latin word for love. He is depicted as a winged young man or a boy, surrounded by flowers, sometimes playing a lyre, and more often with a bow and arrows.

The arrows he uses to pierce the hearts of his victims (gods and mortals alike) are said to be made of gold or bronze, with a sharp point that can cause intense longing, love, or make the victim irresistible to another.

Cupid's mother is Venus (the goddess of love), and his father is Mars (the god of war). His father is not always mentioned, but it is perhaps implied by Cupid's earlier association with battle, conflict, chaos, and mayhem. Cupid's Greek equivalent is Eros, who had a different parentage. According to Hesiod he was the fourth being to emerge into existence at the beginning of creation.

Cupid often appears in mythology as a narrative force which serves to set the story in motion. In art, Cupid sometimes appears in multiples as the the Amores or the Amorini. This is similar to the Greek multiples of Eros known as the Erotes.

After millennia of mythology and art, Cupid remains an iconic symbol of romantic love and passion, often used in the arts, and popular culture. His image is instantly recognisable, and his association with love, desire, and romance has become an integral part of collective cultural imagination.

Diana (The Chaste Huntress and Protector)

Roman Name(s): Diana
Greek Name(s): *Αρτεμις*, Artemis
Etruscan Name(s): Artume

Diana is the goddess of chastity, childbirth, midwifery, hunting, wild animals, the moon, the wilderness, and protector of young women. She is a personification of multiple ideals of femininity and youthful feminine strength, skill, and chastity. As a symbol of chastity, she is one of the three major virgin goddesses alongside Minerva and Vesta.

The moment she was born from her mother Latona, she then assisted in the delivery of her twin brother Apollo, and she is therefore associated with childbirth and midwifery.

Diana and her twin brother Apollo both symbolise archery, hunting, and the protection of the young. Accompanied by her band of nymphs, the Pleiades (daughters of Pleione), Diana roams the forests and the wilderness while hunting, sometimes at night, by the light of the moon. This led to her being associated with the moon, and with the goddess of the moon Luna. There are Roman Imperial copies of statues dedicated to Diana-Luna which combine the characteristics of the two goddesses into one, the originals of which date back to the 4th century BCE.

As well as a protector of the young, Diana is capable of severely punishing those who offend her. She has the power to bring ill-health and deadly plague with her arrows. Diana is also seen as a protector of modesty, as exemplified in the cautionary tale of Actaeon, the young hunter in the woods who sees Diana bathing naked. This angers Diana greatly, and she punishes him by turning him into a deer, after which he is then devoured by his own hunting dogs, who no longer recognise him as their master. In art and literature, this myth has been depicted in various ways, often with Actaeon being shown as a deer being chased by his own hounds. The story has also been used as a metaphor for the dangers of pride and the consequences of hubris.

Diana is one of the most widely venerated of the ancient Roman deities, with temples, altars, and shrines throughout ancient Rome. Before the days of the Roman Empire and the Roman Republic, when Rome was a kingdom, a temple for the worship of Diana was built during the reign of the king Servius Tullius in the 6th century BCE. Often depicted with a bow and a quiver of arrows, the astrological symbol for Diana is the initial D which on one hand represents the crescent moon, and on the other hand represents a bow with an arrow.

Diana is one of the *Dii Selecti* (the chosen gods), a list of the twenty principal gods of Roman religion according to Varro (recorded by Augustine of Hippo in his work De Civitate Dei or The City of God in the 5th century CE). According to Varro, who was of Sabine origin, Diana was originally worshipped by the Sabines in the Central *Apennine* Mountains before being adopted by the Romans.

Dies (The Day)

Roman Name(s): Dies
Greek Name(s): Ἡμερα, Hêmera, Hemera

Dies is the personification of the day. Each morning she disperses the mists of the night, reveals the shining blue ether of the day, and helps to bring light and warmth to the world.

According to Hyginus, Chaos and Caligo are the parents of Nox (Night), Dies (Day), Scotus (Darkness), and Aether (Heavenly Light). Then Aether and Dies are the parents of Terra (The Earth) and Mare (The Sea).

According to Cicero, Aether and Dies are the parents of Caelus (The Sky). Then Dies and Caelus are the parents of Mercury.

As a personification, Dies is more of a divine substance rather than an anthropomorphic goddess; however the gods and goddesses became increasingly depicted in human form over time.

There is little evidence of Dies ever having her own cult in ancient times, however there is archaeological evidence of her worship being combined with that of Sol (the god of the sun).

The worship of the sun and the daylight in the ancient world contained several themes: Light and illumination, purification and cleansing, renewal and rebirth (the daily setting and rising of the sun, the daily return of the dawn), the cycles of nature, etc.

Dies became more and more identified with Aurora (The Dawn), until finally Dies's role was replaced by Aurora, and they became identified as one and the same.

Discordia (Strife and Discord)

Roman Name(s): Discordia
Greek Name(s): *Ερις*, Eris
Etruscan Name(s): Eris

Discordia is the personification of discord, strife, contention, and rivalry. Her name translates literally as discord, and her Greek equivalent is Eris. She is often depicted as a beautiful but troublesome goddess, known for causing quarrels and conflicts between the gods and mortals.

Discordia is the one who threw the golden apple into the wedding of Peleus and Thetis, which led to the Judgment of Paris and the Trojan War. The apple was inscribed with the word 'Kallisti' (Greek: Καλλίστη), which means "to the fairest". Everyone argued about who was the fairest and who the golden apple was intended for, which caused a great deal of strife. The golden apple is a symbol of Discordia's power and influence.

In the Homeric tradition, Discordia is portrayed as the spirit of the strife and discord of war. She accompanies Mars on the battlefield, delighting in the havoc and human bloodshed created, long after all others have left. This has led to her being closely associated with the goddess of war Bellona, whom the Greeks knew as Enyo.

In Hesiod's Theogony (226-232) Eris (Discordia) is described as the mother of a variety of allegorical beings representing the causes of humankind's misfortune: Labour, Forgetfulness, Starvation, Pains, Fighting, Battle, Manslaughter, Quarrels, Lies, Stories, Disputes, Anarchy, and the breaking of Oaths. In Hesiod's Works and Days (11-24) he argues that there are two kinds of Strife, the first representing war, the second representing the discord and strife associated with man's jealousy and competition with his neighbour.

Egeria (Water Nymph of Laws and Rituals)

Roman Name(s): Egeria, Aegeria
Etruscan Name(s): Vegoia

Egeria is the giver of laws and rituals, and a water nymph, a minor deity or supernatural being that inhabits bodies of water, such as rivers, lakes, and oceans.

Like all water nymphs, she is depicted as beautiful, seductive, alluring, not only connected to the natural world, but also able to control the tides, manipulate the weather, and communicate with creatures, mortals, and gods.

Egeria plays an important role in the early history of Rome as the divine consort and counsellor of the second king of Rome, Numa Pompilius, who succeeded Rome's founder Romulus. Egeria advised Numa Pompilius in the ways of the laws and rituals that became the basis of ancient Roman religion.

She was worshipped at sacred groves, such as the sacred site of Nemi at Aricia in the region of Latium. The source of water at the site was dedicated to the exclusive use of the priestesses of Vesta, also known as the Vestal Virgins.

Egeria gave wisdom and prophecy in return for libations (ritual pouring of liquids dedicated to a deity) of water or milk at her sacred groves.

She is also thought of as a prophetess and an author of sacred books, similar to the Etruscan goddess Vegoia, who is believed to have written books of prophecy such as the Libri Fulgurales, which were used to interpret the will of the gods through lightning strikes.

Empanda (Sanctuary and Protection)

Roman Name(s): Empanda, Panda
Oscan Name(s): Patanai
Umbrian Name(s): Padellar

Empanda or Panda is an ancient goddess who offers asylum, sanctuary, protection, food, and water to those in need. Her name is interpreted by ancient scholars as a combination of *pandere* = to open, and *panem dare* = to give bread.

Varro notes that there is a Roman gate named after her. In the original fortifications of the Capitoline Hill at Rome, one of the gateways was named *Porta Pandana*. This gate is also mentioned in the Iguvine Tablets (VIa 14) in the ancient Umbrian language as *Pertome Padellar*. Modern scholars have also associated the Latin name Empanda with the ancient Oscan name *Patani*.

The Roman writer Sextus Pompeius Festus describes her as a *dea paganorum* = a goddess of those in the fields (Interestingly the word pagan in this context became a derogatory term meaning someone from the fields or the outer districts who was uneducated, but later as Christianity spread throughout the Roman Empire, the word took on the meaning of someone who was uneducated in the ways of Christ).

Varro also associates Empanda with Ceres, the goddess of agriculture, grain, produce, etc. which opens the possibility that Empanda evolved into Ceres, or Empanda was replaced by Ceres, either way to become an equivalent of the Greek goddess Demeter. Some scholars have theorised that Empanda or Panda are in fact epithets that were given to the goddess Juno.

Epona (Protector of Horses)

Roman Name(s): Epona
Celtic Name(s): Epona, Epane

Epona is the goddess and protector of horses, ponies, donkies, and mules. She was originally worshipped by the Celtic people of Gaul (present day France, Belgium, Germany, and Switzerland).

In Celtic mythology, she was considered a powerful patron of horses, agriculture, livestock, and also a goddess of fertility.

She is often depicted as a female figure riding a horse or standing beside one or two horses. It is also possible that with her horses she was seen as the leader of souls on the journey into the afterlife.

There is evidence that the Celts of the Iberian Peninsula, known as Celtiberians, made a dedication to *Epane* which was discovered at an archaeological site at Mount Bernorio in the provice of Palencia, in northern Spain.

Rome's conquest of Gaul in the 1st century BCE resulted in its Romanisation under Roman rule as the province of Gallia.

It was only the goddess Epona that was adopted and worshipped outside of the region across the Roman Empire as a patroness of cavalry.

She was often invoked by soldiers and travellers seeking protection and safe passage for them and their horses. Epona's feast day in the Roman calendar was on the 18th day of December.

Falacer (Ancient God of the Sky)

Roman Name(s): Falacer, Divus Pater Falacer
Etruscan Name(s): Falandum

Falacer is an ancient god worshipped by the Latinii, and possibly the Etruscans, the Sabines, and other Italic tribes across the Italian peninsula.

The Roman grammarian Sextus Pompeius Festus, active in the later 2nd century CE, considers Falacer to be an epithet or aspect of Jupiter (the god of the sky). This could indicate that Falacer is perhaps an earlier version of Jupiter of Etruscan origin, and that he was absorbed from the Etruscans into the Roman pantheon as an epithet or aspect of Jupiter.

Festus adds that Falacer's name comes from the word *falandum*, which is the Etruscan word for heaven. In the same way, perhaps Fallandum is an earlier primordial personification of the sky that was absorbed as an epithet or aspect of Tinia, the Etruscan god of the sky and equivalent of Jupiter.

The ancient Roman village of Falacrine (*Falacrinum* or *Phalacrina*) in the Sabine hill country northeast of Rome is possibly named after Falacer, or possibly Falacer was originally cultivated as the god and protector of the village, which is also said to be the birthplace of the Roman Emperor Vespasian.

The name Falacer is also correlated with the the city of Falerii and the Falisci, an Italic tribe who may have worshipped Falacer as the eponymous ancestor of their tribe.

Falacer is named as one of the minor *Dii Flaminales*, gods who were cultivated by flamines, special priests who were assigned to the official cults during the Roman Republic.

Fatum (Impending Doom)

Roman Name(s): Fatum, Olethrus
Greek Name(s): *Μορος*, Moros, *Ολεθρος*, Olethros

Fatum is the personification of doom, the personified spirit of the impending force that drives mortals to their ultimate fate. His name translates as doom, fate, ruin, and calamity.

Also translating from the name Olethrus is the word bane, an archaic word of Old English origin meaning something which causes death, especially poison.

Among his siblings collectively known as the Children of Nox are: the Parcae (the Three Fates), Mors (the god of peaceful death), and the Tenebrae (the spirits of death on the battlefield).

Hesiod describes Fatum as bring born of Nyx (Nox) without a father, whereas Hyginus and Cicero name Scotus (Erebus) as his father.

Fatum also has the power to enable mortals to foresee their impending fate. The Greeks knew Fatum as Moros, and also the name Olethros (*Ολεθρος*).

Aeschylus writes in Prometheus Bound that Prometheus gave humanity the spiritess of hope called Elpis (Spes), or the spiritesses the Elpides (The Hopes) in order help humanity to ignore Fatum.

Fatum is also referred to by Aeschylus as "the all-destroying god, who, even in the realm of Death, does not set his victim free".

Faunus (The Wild Forests)

Roman Name(s): Faunus, Inuus
Greek Name(s): Πάν, Pán, Pan

Faunus is the rustic god of the forests, plains, countryside, and fields. He has the power to make cattle fertile, and in this aspect he is called Inuus. He is of Indo-European origin, and possibly related to the Vedic god Rudra. He was worshipped by Roman farmers long before joining the Roman pantheon as a nature deity. Faunus has a counterpart called Fauna, who is variously described as his wife, sister, or daughter. There are also the Fauni, a large group of Fauns who are the spirits of various places of untamed woodland, of which Faunus is their leader.

Before the influence of Greek mythology on Roman mythology in the 3rd and 2nd centuries BCE, Faunus was not originally depicted with horns like his Greek equivalent Pan, but when they became idenfitied as one and the same god, Faunus then became depicted with horns.

Virgil described Faunus as the legendary king of the Latins, the Italic tribe in the original ancient region of Latium where Rome was founded, and where the Latin language gets its name from.

Varro in his *De Lingua Latina* (7.36) states that Faunus revealed the future in dreams and voices to those who came to sleep in his sacred groves and precincts, lying on the fleeces of sacrificed lambs.

The two festivals of Faunalia were celebrated on the 13th day of February in the temple of Faunus on the island in the Tiber, and on the 5th December when people left offerings in the temple and took part in dances.

Februus (Purification, and the Underworld)

Roman Name(s): Februus, Febris
Etruscan Name(s): Februus

Februus is an ancient Italic god of purification, who was worshipped by the Romans and the Etruscans. He was also worshipped as the god of the Underworld by the Etruscans. For them he was also a god of riches (money and gold) and death.

The connection to wealth and the Underworld is in the name Plouton, which is of Greek origin meaning the wealthy one, used as a euphemistic name by Greeks who had a superstitious aversion to calling Hades by his actual name. This nickname was used by the Romans for their version of the god of the Underworld whose name was Pluto.

Februus may have been replaced by the god Febris, the goddess of fever. The sweating of fevers is perhaps thought of symbolically as a purgative process, necessitating washing and purification.

Februus is also possibly named in honor of Februa or Februalia, a festival of washing and purification held on the 15th of the holy month of Februarius, where the name of the month February comes from.

Februus is named as one of the *Dii Inferi* (the gods below), the shadowy collective of ancient Roman deities associated with death and the Underworld.

Feronia (The Wilderness, Fertility, and Abundance)

Roman Name(s): Feronia

Feronia is an ancient Italic goddess of the wilderness, wildlife, fertility, health, and abundance.

She was worshipped by the Etruscans, Faliscans, and the Sabines before being adopted into the ancient Roman religion.

Her name comes from the Sabine adjective *fer* similar to the Latin *ferus* meaning uncultivated, untamed, of the fields, of the woods, which is where the English word feral comes from.

The Sabines also believed that she had powers of prophecy, and that she was a goddess of travellers, fire, and the waters.

Private individuals of the Sabine community were permitted to mint money, and Feronia was among the deities that were placed on their coins to honour their heritage.

According to Titus Livius (Livy), the Latins worshipped Feronia as a goddess of the harvest, and thus she represented the gifts of nature and their cultivation into that which was useful and nourishing to the people.

According to Servius the Grammarian, she also granted freedom to slaves and civil rights to the most humble in society. Her festival Feroniae was held on the 13th day of November.

Livy stated that freed slave women collected money as a gift for Feronia. Some sources state that slaves were set free at her temple near Terracina.

Servius writes that when a fire destroyed the woods near Terracina, the locals were moving the statues to another location, when the burnt wood suddenly turned green.

According to Pliny, all attempts at building towers between her sanctuary and nearby Terracina were a failure, because all of them were destroyed by lightning. This was interpreted as a powerful sign from Feronia that the wilderness around her sanctuary should not be built around and should be kept in the wild.

Inscriptions to Feronia are found mostly in central Italy, and her shrines are located in the wild, far from human settlements.

Varro, who was of Sabine origin, confirms that Feronia was originally worshipped by the Sabines in the Central Apennine Mountains before being adopted by the Romans.

Fides (Trust, Faith, and Credibility)

Roman Name(s): Fides, Bona Fides

Fides is a goddess of trust, faithfulness, good faith (*bona fides*). Fides was one of the original virtues to be cultivated as a divinity with ceremonies and temples. For the Romans, Fides embodied everything that was needed for the honour and credibility of Rome, from fidelity in marriage, to contractual arrangements, and the obligation owed by soldiers to Rome.

Fides also symbolised reliability, people working together towards the common good, and forming strong credible bonds between people and their communities. This is where the English word fidelity comes from.

The concept of *Fides Publica Populi Romani* (public trust of the Roman people) is symbolised by the legend of Marcus Atilius Regulus, a consul during the first Punic War who was captured by the Carthaginians in the battle of Tunis in 255 BCE.

After several years in captivity, he was sent back to Rome to negotiate a peace treaty and argue for Carthaginian terms, and to only return if the talks were unsuccessful. He instead advised the Roman Senate against accepting the terms as they were unfavourable, and that the war could still be won.

Despite all pleadings, Regulus then put the needs of the Roman Republic above his own interests, and returned to Carthage to deliver the rejection of terms, heroically sacrificing himself to his certain fate.

According to Varro, who was of Sabine origin, Fides was originally worshipped by the Sabines in the Central Apennine Mountains before being adopted by the Romans.

Flora (Spring, Flowers, and New Growth)

Roman Name(s): Flora
Greek Name(s): Χλωρις, Khlôris, Chloris
Oscan Name(s): Fluusa

Flora is the goddess of flowers and a nymph of the Islands of the Blessed, a realm of the Elysian Fields which is the final resting place of the souls of heroes and virtuous people.

Her Greek equivalent is Chloris. Ovid's Fasti (194-198) reads as follows:

"(dum loquitur, vernas emat ab ore rosas):
Chloris eram, quae Flora vocor: corrupta Latino
nominis est nostri littera Graeca sono.
Chloris eram, nymphe campi felicis, ubi audis
rem fortunatis ante fuisse viris,"

"(While she spoke, her lips breathed out vernal roses):
I, called Flora now, was Chloris: the first letter in Greek
Of my name, became corrupted in the Latin language.
I was Chloris, a nymph of those happy fields,
Where, as you've heard, fortunate men once lived,"

Flora was abducted by Favonius (the West Wind), which is a parallel to the story of his brother Aquilo (the North Wind) who abducted the Athenian princess Orithyia. Flora and Favonius produced a son called Carpus who is associated with fertility and springtime.

According to Ovid, Flora was also thought to have been responsible for the transformations of Adonis, Attis, Crocus, Hyacinthus, and Narcissus into flowers.

Flora was also partially responsible for the creation of Mars, who Juno gave birth to in revenge for Jupiter fathering Minerva. Using a flower, Flora made Juno pregnant with Mars, and Flora was given a place in Rome as a reward.

Flora is identified with the Oscan goddess of flowers Fluusa, which is evidence that her cult was widespread among the Italic peoples as well as the Greeks. The astrological symbol for Flora is a flower. Her festival Floralia was held between the 28th April and 3rd May and symbolised the renewal of the cycle of life. The festival began in 240 BCE, and in 238 BCE she was given a temple. For five days people would wear flowers and bright happy costumes, and farces and mimes were enacted.

Flora is one of the minor *Dii Flaminales*, gods who were cultivated by flamines, special priests who were assigned to the official cults during the Roman Republic.

According to Varro, who was of Sabine origin, Flora was originally worshipped by the Sabines in the Central *Apennine* Mountains before being adopted by the Romans.

Fontus (Wells and Springs)

Roman Name(s): Fontus, Fons

Fontus is the god of wells and springs in ancient Roman religion. A religious festival called the Fontinalia was held on the the 13th day of October in his honour. Throughout the city of Rome, fountains and well heads were adorned with garlands.

He is the son of Juturna (the goddess of fountains, wells, and springs) and Janus (the god of boundaries, thresholds, and doorways). The second king of Rome, Numa Pompilius, is believed to have been buried near the altar of Fontus (*ara Fontis*) on the Janiculan Hill in Rome.

Fontus, his mother Juturna, and the Tempestates (gods of storms and sudden weather) were all honoured with cults that were founded between 259 and 241 BCE.

Water as a source of regeneration was a symbol in Mithraism, and in various temples of Mithras, collectively known as mithraea, inscriptions to Fons Perennis (eternal spring, or unfailing stream) have been found.

In one of the scenes from the story of Mithras, he strikes a rock, which then flows with water. A mithraic text explains that the stream was a source of life-giving water and immortal refreshment.

According to Varro, who was of Sabine origin, Fons was originally worshipped by the Sabines in the Central Apennine Mountains before being adopted by the Romans.

Fortuna (Fortune and Luck)

Roman Name(s): Fortuna
Greek Name(s): *Τυχη*, Tykhê, Tyche
Etruscan Name(s): Nortia

Fortuna is the goddess of fortune, chance, providence, and fate. Her Greek equivalent is Tyche. She is the daughter of Oceanus (the god of the waters) and Tethys (the goddess of the waters), and therefore one of the Oceanids. As well as personal fate, Fortuna presides over the fate of communities, towns, and cities.

Sometimes she is named as a daughter of Jupiter in other sources, and described as bringing positive messages to people relating to external events outside their control.

She is often depicted with a rudder or a ship's wheel, symbolising her influence on the course of events, literally steering a course. The ship's wheel is also the wheel of fortune representing the cyclical nature of fortune and misfortune.

In the time of Alexander the Great, the positive and negative whims of fate were embodied as much by Fortuna as the Twelve Olympians. The Greek historian Polybius believed that when no cause could be discovered for events such as floods, droughts, or frosts, then the cause may be attributed to Tyche (Fortuna).

She is associated with the goddess Invidia or Invidentia, who restores a sense of balance by bringing loss upon those who have been favoured too generously by Fortuna. They became increasingly worshipped side by side, sharing cult status either as two equal opposite deities, or with one being an aspect of the other.

Resurgences of the worship of Fortuna often occurred during times of instability and uncertain change, where those fearful of the future would pray for her to deliver them through difficult times. By contrast, poets of the ages would lament and bemoan her sudden and unaccountable changes of mood or behaviour. She is addressed in the anonymous goliardic poem O Fortuna written around the 13th century in the monastery of Benediktbeuern, in southern Germany.

> *"O Fortuna velut luna statu variabilis,*
>
> *semper crescis aut decrescis; vita detestabilis*
> *nunc obdurat et tunc curat ludo mentis aciem,*
> *egestatem, potestatem dissolvit ut glaciem."*

> "O Fortune, like the moon you are changeable,
>
> ever waxing ever waning; hateful life
>
> first oppresses and then soothes playing with mental clarity;
> poverty and power it melts them like ice."

According to Varro, who was of Sabine origin, Fortuna was originally worshipped by the Sabines in the Central Apennine Mountains before being adopted by the Romans.

Furrina (Springs and Runnning Water)

Roman Name(s): Furrina, Furina

Furrina is an ancient goddess who had become relatively obscure by the 1st century BCE. Her cult dates back to the earliest period of Roman religious history.

Furrina is one of the minor *Dii Flaminales*, gods who were cultivated by flamines, special priests who were assigned to the official cults during the Roman Republic.

The little we know about Furrina indicates that she is associated with water. Her name is related to the moving or bubbling of water.

The word furrina is related to the Gothic word brunna (spring). The Latin word fervere means to boil, which is also where the English words fervent and effervescent come from.

Furrina had a sacred spring and a shrine in Rome on the southwestern slopes of the Janiculan Hill on the right bank of the Tiber. At the site there are inscriptions dedicated to the *nymphae furrinae* (the nymphs of Furrina) which remain today as a grove within the gardens of Villia Sciarra.

The festival of Furrinalia was held on the 25th day of July in the Roman calendar, alongside Lucania (the festival of groves, 17th and 19th July), and Neptunalia (Neptune, god of the waters, 23rd July), all grouped together under the theme of woods and running waters, a relief from the heat of July.

Genius (Spirit of Divine Nature)

Roman Name(s): Genius, Genii

A Genius (plural: Genii) is a minor deity that serves as a guardian for a place, a person, a group, activity, or an object. The concept is comparable to a guardian angel, in that a Genius follows each person from the hour of their birth until the end of their life.

A specific place would have a *genius loci* (genius of the place), which if invoked or gained favour with, could make events in that place fortuitous or successful.

Christian theologian Augustine of Hippo in his *De civitate Dei* (the City of God) (VII. 13) compares the Christian soul to the Roman genius:

"Et cum alio loco genium dicit esse uniuscuiusque animum rationalem et ideo esse singulos singulorum, talem autem mundi animum Deum esse: ad hoc idem utique reuocat, ut tamquam uniuersalis genius ipse mundi animus esse credatur. Hic est igitur quem appellant Iouem."

"And when in another place he says that Genius is the rational soul of every one, and therefore exists separately in each individual, but that the corresponding soul of the world is God, he just comes back to this same thing — namely, that the soul of the world itself is to be held to be, as it were, the universal genius. This, therefore, is what he calls Jupiter."

Augustine of Hippo also records that Genius is one of the *Dii Selecti* (the chosen gods), a list of the twenty principal gods of Roman religion, according to Varro.

The Gratiae (The Graces)

Roman Name(s): Gratia, Gratiae
Greek Name(s): Charis, Charites

The Gratiae are three or more goddesses of charm, beauty, nature, human creativity, goodwill, and fertility. The ancient Greeks called them the Charites (Χάριτες), and the Romans recognised them as the Gratiae (the Graces). They are the daughters of Jupiter and Eurynome (also varyingly named as Eunomia, Eurydome, or Eurymedousa, and Euanthe).

Their main function is to attend to the gods, especially during feasts and dances. They are the companions of Venus and are said to weave or dye her traditional dress known as a *peplos* (πέπλος). The Gratiae are also associated with the Underworld and the Eleusinian Mysteries, in which the journey to and from the Underworld is part of the symbolism of death and rebirth.

Hesiod names the Gratiae as Aglaea ('shining), Euphrosyne (joy), and Thalia (blooming). Aglaea (also known as Charis) is the youngest of the three and the wife of Hephaestus (Vulcan).

Among their many varying names are: • Antheia (Blossoms) • Auxesia ('spring Growth) • Auxo (Growth, Increase) • Charis (Grace) • Cleta (Renowned, Sound) • Damia (Earth Mother) • Eudaimonia (Happiness) • Eupheme (Good Omen) • Euphrosyne (Good Cheer, Joy, Mirth) • Euthymia (Good Mood) • Eutychia (Good Luck) • Hegemone (Leader, Queen) • Kale (Beauty) • Paidia (Play) • Pandaisia (Banquet) • Pannychis (Night Festivities) • Paregoros (Consolation) • Pasithea (Hallucination, Relaxation) • Peitho (Persuasion) • Phaenna (Bright, Light)

Hermaphroditus (The Ancient Androgynous One)

Hermaphroditus, Herculaneum fresco 1–50 CE
National Archaeological Museum, Naples
Wikipedia Creative Commons, Public Domain

Roman Name(s): Hermaphroditus, Atlantius
Greek Name(s): Ἑρμαφρόδιτος, Hermaphróditos, Ατλαντιάδης, Atlantiades

Hermaphroditus is the child of Hermes (Mercury) and Aphrodite (Venus). His name is a combination of Hermes + Aphrodite = Hermaphroditus.

Hermaphroditus's father Hermes is the son of Maia, and Maia is the daughter of Atlas. This means that Hermaphroditus is the great-grandchild of Atlas, and for this reason, he is sometimes called Atlantius by the Romans, and Atlantiades by the Greeks.

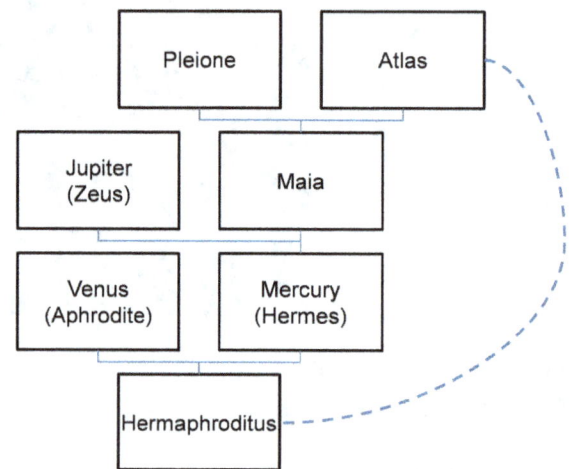

According to Ovid, Hermaphroditus was a beautiful young man who was nursed in the caves of Mount Ida by naiads (female spirits of fountains and fresh water). One day he grew bored of his surroundings and wished to go travelling. One day, in the woods of Caria near Halicarnassus, he encountered the naiad called Salmacis in her pool, and she was overcome with lust for him. She tried to flirt with him but he rejected her. However, she would not take no for an answer, and forced herself upon him. While he struggled to free himself, she cried out to the gods that they should never be parted. The gods heard this, and in answer to her prayers, they were both merged into one single being, a hermaphrodite, which is the origin of the word.

Hermaphroditus is named as one of the many winged gods of love and desire that accompany Venus. These many winged gods are known by the Romans as the Cupidines or Amores, and they are known by the Greeks as the Erotes.

Hermaphroditus has long been a symbol of androgyny or effeminacy in the ancient Roman and Greek world, often portrayed in art as a female figure with male genitals. The Greek philosopher Theophrastus suggests a link between Hermaphroditus and the institution of marriage, as Hermaphrotidus embodies both masculine and feminine qualities, he symbolises the coming together of men and women in sacred union. His parents are also associated with protecting and blessing brides.

Honos (Honour, Valour, and Bravery)

Roman Name(s): Honos

Honos is the Roman god personifying honour. Honos is closely associated with the goddess Virtus who personifies bravery and virtue. Thus, honour and virtue were important ideals for the Romans, particularly concerning valour and bravery on the battlefield.

Honos is commonly depicted with a laurel wreath, holding an olive branch, or holding a cornucopia (a horn of plenty). The Aureus was a Roman gold coin worth 25 silver denarii, and has been known to depict Honos holding an olive branch and a cornucopia; it was issued from the 1st century BCE to the beginning of the 4th century CE until it was replaced by the *Solidus*.

In 234 BCE, a temple was dedicated to Honos outside the Porta Capena, one of the main gates to the city of Rome, following the Roman victory over the Ligurians in the north.

In 222 BCE, after the Roman victory at the Battle of Clastidium, Roman General and politician Marcus Claudius Marcellus vowed to build a temple to Honos.

In 212 BCE, after the capture of Syracuse and gaining control over the whole island of Sicily, Marcus Claudius Marcellus renewed his vow. During the Second Punic War he restored the temple of Honos, and built a second adjoining shrine to Virtus, making it a double temple, finally dedicated after his death by his son in 205 BCE. The temple was again restored by Vespasian, who ruled from 69 to 79 CE, after which it remained standing well into the fourth century CE.

Another temple to Honus and Virtus was built by Gaius Marius after the Roman victory in the Cimbrian war in 101 BCE. It was built using the spoils captured from the defeated Cimbri and the Teutones.

Invidia, Invidentia (Divine Retributive Justice)

Roman Name(s): Invidia, Invidentia, Nemesis, Rivalitas
Greek Name(s): Νεμεσις, Nemesis, Ῥαμνουσία, Rhamnousia

Invidia is the goddess or personification of retribution, retributive justice, vengeance, and punishment of hubris, arrogance before the gods, evil deeds, and ill-deserved good fortune. She is an agent of the moral reverence for natural law.

Her name means she who distributes or deals out what is due. She is a winged goddess depicted with a wide range of icons, such as an apple branch, balancing scales, a bridle, a dagger, a lash, a measuring rod, a rein, a sand-clock or timer, a sword, or a whip. She was referred to as Invidia or Invidentia (Jealousy), and Rivalitas (Rivalry), but the Greeks knew her as Nemesis.

Happiness and unhappiness is measured out by her, making sure that happiness is not too frequent or too excessive, to maintain equilibrium. She punishes and levels the balance by bringing about losses and suffering, sometimes as a check against the extravagant favours of the goddess Fortuna (Fortuna) or Tyche (Luck).

Hesiod and Pausanias both suggest that Invidia was born of Nox (the goddess of the night) with no father, whereas Hyginus and Cicero name Scotus (the god of darkness) as her father. Oceans and Jupiter are also suggested as her father in other sources.

Invidia is sometimes given the name Adrasteia (the inescapable) by the writers of Adrastus who according to Strabo built the first sanctuary of Nemesis (Invidia) on the river Asopus. She is also given the name Rhamnousia because of the temple dedicated to her at Rhamnos in Attica according to Pausanias.

Iris (The Rainbow Messenger)

Roman Name(s): Iris, Arcus
Greek Name(s): *Ιρις*, Iris

Iris is the goddess of the rainbow and the messenger of the Olympian gods. She is often described as the handmaiden and personal messenger of Juno. The ancient Greek name Îris (*Ιρις*) translates both as rainbow and the halo of the moon. She is the daughter of Thaumas (a personification of the sea), and Electra (one of the three thousand Oceanids, water-nymphs).

Iris is depicted as a winged young woman, sometimes carrying a caduceus (a symbol of a divine messenger, a staff entwined with two snakes), and sometimes a pitcher which she uses to serve the gods nectar or water. She is the consort of Favonius (The West Wind), and together they produced Pothus, one of the Cupides (Love Spirits) who accompanies Venus.

Iris has the power to travel with the speed of the wind from one end of the world to the other, and into the depths of the Kingdom of the Sea and the Underworld. Some say that Iris travels on the rainbow when delivering messages from the gods to mortals on earth.

There are no known temples, shrines, or sanctuaries dedicated to Iris, nor any festivals held in her honour. She does appear to have been worshipped or at least sacrificed to by the people of Delos, offering her a cheesecake called *basyniae*, a type of cake of wheatflour, suet, and honey boiled together.

Iris has been given many poetic titles and epithets, including golden-winged, swift-footed, wind-swift-footed, dewy, daughter of Thaumas, wondrous one, storm-footed, and storm-swift.

Janus (Beginnings, Openings, and Transitions)

Roman Name(s): Janus, Ianus, Ianvs
Etruscan Name(s): Culsans

Janus is the god of beginnings, gates, transitions, time, duality, doorways, passages, frames, and endings. The Latin word *ianua* or *janua* variously translates as door, gate, entrance, and opening. The month of January is connected to Janus (*Januarius*). He is also known with the epithets *Janus Pater* = Janus Father, and *Janus Bifrons* = Janus two-fronts or Janus two-faces. He is usually depicted with two faces, sometimes both the same age, sometimes one young and one old, sometimes with one face looking into the past and the other looking into the future.

As a god who presides over the beginnings and endings of things, Janus is very much a symbol of duality and cycles in all things. He presides over the beginnings and the ends of conflicts, and therefore represents the duality of war and peace.

Janus was associated with the god Portunus, a small god representing harbours and gateways, small because of the diminutive *-unus* on the word *porta* meaning gate, door, etc.

While there is no known Greek equivalent of Janus, the Etruscans knew him as Culsans. Evidence of Culsans is limited to the 3rd and 2nd centuries BCE, and many artefacts found have come from the city of Cortona in Etruria (modern day Arezzo, Tuscany).

Janus is one of the *Dii Selecti* (the chosen gods), a list of the twenty principal gods of Roman religion according to Varro (recorded by Augustine of Hippo in his work De Civitate Dei or The City of God in the 5th century CE).

Juno (Queen of the Gods)

Roman Name(s): Juno
Greek Name(s): Ἥρη, Hêrê, Hera
Etruscan Name(s): Uni

Juno is the Queen of the Gods and of Mount Olympus, the goddess of marriage, the sky and the stars of heaven, and the protector of women.

She is depicted as a beautiful woman wearing a crown and holding a sceptre tipped with a lotus, and accompanied by a lion, a cuckoo, or a hawk.

Juno's sacred animal is the peacock, and the astrological symbols for Juno and her Greek equivalent Hera represent a peacock with a cross at the bottom.

She is a dignified matronly figure, upright, enthroned, sometimes wearing a high cylindrical crown known as a *polos* or a *diadem*, and veiled as a married woman.

Juno is known for her jealous and vengeful nature in punishing those who wrong her, particularly Jupiter's many adulterous lovers and illegitimate offspring.

She is the patron goddess of lawful marriage who presides over weddings, blesses and legalises marital unions, and protects women during childbirth. She is sometimes shown holding a pomegranate as an emblem of immortality.

Before Juno's marriage to Jupiter, she was a maternal goddess associated with cattle, given the epithet Boôpis by Homer translated as cow-eyed. This is similar to the Ancient Egyptian goddess Hathor who is also a maternal goddess associated with cattle.

Juno had an important role as the protector, special counsellor, and patron goddess of Rome and the Roman Empire. She is often given the epithet *Regina* (queen) and is a member of the Capitoline Triad, three deities (Jupiter, Juno, and Minerva) with a special elaborate temple on Rome's Capitoline Hill holding a central place in the public religion of Rome. This is remarkably similar to, and perhaps derived from, the Etruscan trio or trinity of Tinia (Jupiter), Uni (Juno), and Menrva (Minerva).

Juno's Etruscan equivalent Uni was also the patron goddess of Perugia in the ancient region of Umbria. The Roman historian Livy states that Juno (Uni) was an important goddess in the ancient Etruscan city of Veii, who was adopted into the Roman pantheon after Veii was sacked in 396 BCE.

Juno is one of the *Dii Selecti* (the chosen gods), a list of the twenty principal gods of Roman religion according to Varro (recorded by Augustine of Hippo in his work De Civitate Dei or The City of God in the 5th century CE).

Jupiter (King of the Gods)

Roman Name(s): Jupiter, Jove
Greek Name(s): Ζευς, Zeus
Etruscan Name(s): Tinia

Jupiter is the King of the Gods, the ruler of the skies, the weather, law and order, destiny, fate, and kingship. He is also called the sky father. His Greek equivalent is Zeus.

He is often depicted with a royal sceptre, an eagle (a sign of immortality), and holding a lightning bolt which was fashioned for him as a weapon by the Cyclopes.

He was the youngest child of Saturn (the god of time) and Ops (the queen of the heavens). Saturn, having overthrown his own father Caelus, feared being overthrown by his offspring, and took to devouring them as soon as they were born.

When Ops bore her sixth child Jupiter, she had the infant Jupiter spirited away by the nymph Amalthea to the island of Crete, and Saturn was tricked into swallowing a stone wrapped in swaddling bands believing it to be Jupiter.

Jupiter's mother appointed three, five, or nine rustic spirits called the Curetes or the Dactyli to guard Jupiter in a cave on Mount Ida. They drowned out his infant cries with their dancing and the clashing of their shields and spears. When Jupiter reached manhood, he was assisted by Metis in rescuing his siblings. Metis gave Saturn an emetic, making Saturn vomit back up all of the infant gods he had devoured (and the stone).

Jupiter together with his siblings eventually defeated and overthrew their father Saturn and the Titans during the Titanomachy (the ten year war between the Olympians and the Titans for the control of the cosmos). Jupiter banished the Titans to Tartarus beneath the earth and at the bottom of the Underworld, and then became the ruler of the new generation of Olympian gods, and the supreme ruler of the cosmos.

Jupiter is also well known for fathering many divine and heroic offspring within and outside of his marriages, including Agdistis, Aigipan, Aletheia, Aphrodite, Apollo, Ares, Artemis, Asopos, Ate, Athena, Britomartis, The Cabeiroi, Caerus, The Charites, Dionysus, Eileithyia, Eris, Ersa, Harmonia, Hebe, Hephaestus, Hermes, The Horai, The Litai, Melinoe, The Moirai, The Muses, Nemea, The Nymphai, The Palikoi, Pan, Pandeia, Proserpina, Phasis, and Zagreus.

Jupiter is one of the *Dii Selecti* (the chosen gods), a list of the twenty principal gods of Roman religion according to author Varro (recorded by Augustine of Hippo in his work De Civitate Dei or The City of God in the 5th century CE).

Jupiter is also one of the major *Dii Flaminales*, gods who were cultivated by flamines, special priests who were assigned to the official cults during the Roman Republic.

Justitia (Divine Order, Justice, and Custom)

Roman Name(s): Justitia
Greek Name(s): Θεμις, Themis, Themis

Justitia is the goddess of justice, divine law and order, morality, righteousness, and custom. She is one of the twelve children of Terra Mater (The Earth) and Caelus (The Sky).

She maintains balance and order in the universe, and she is worshipped and revered as the protector of the innocent and the punisher of the wicked. In this sense, she is a powerful and feared goddess, who will not hesitate to punish to those who break the law or commit injustice or injury to others.

Justitia is the second wife of Jupiter, and is associated with oracles and prophecies, including the Oracle of Delphi. Symbols of Justitia include the scales and the sword of justice. Justitia's most iconic symbol however is the blindfold, which represents her impartiality and inability to be influenced by personal biases or external factors. This symbol is still used today in many legal systems around the world to represent the concept of blind justice.

Justitia is closely associated with Invidia (the goddess of divine retribution) who punishes those who disregard justice. The two goddesses appear together in a shared temple at Rhamnous, with their combined worship demonstrating the importance of their combined roles in keeping divine law and order.

Judges are often referred to as servants of Justice or Lady Justice, and so it is for the maintenance of divine order on Mount Olympus. Juno, the queen of the gods, addresses her politely and respectfully as Lady Justice.

Juturna (Fountains, Wells, and Springs)

Roman Name(s): Juturna, Diuturna

Juturna is a goddess of fountains, wells, and springs. She is also the mother of the god Fontus, whose father is Janus.

Juturna's original home was said to be somewhere on the river Numicius, a river of ancient Latium that flowed into the sea between the towns of Lavinium and Ardea. According to Livy, the Trojan hero Aeneas is buried on the banks of the river Numicius, and according to Ovid, Numicius is the god of the river, who cleanses Aeneas so that he may become a god.

Some myths tell us that Jupiter, the king of the Olympian gods, turned Juturna into a Naiad (a water nymph).

Jupiter then gave Juturna two sacred wells, one in Lavinium, and another near the temple of Vesta in the Forum at Rome known as *Lacus Juturnae* (the Spring of Juturna).

She also had a cult following at Ardea where, with her blessing, the waters were said to be health-giving.

Water nymphs generally preside over a single body of water, but the fact that Jupiter gave Juturna two sacred wells indicates her broader powers and importance, particularly in the region of Latium.

It was at *Lacus Juturnae* that the twin gods Castor and Pollux, known together as Gemini (The Twins), stopped to water their horses while passing through the city of Rome. Castor and Pollux brought news of the Roman victory at the Battle of Lake Regillus in c. 495 BCE, at which they had favoured the Romans and fought on their side in the form of two young horsemen. A temple was built at the site of *Lacus Juturnae* to honour Castor and Pollux, and the Roman victory.

Valerius Maximus, in his *Factorum et Dictorum Memorabilium* (Memorable Facts and Sayings) writes:

> *"Castorem vero et Pollucem etiam illo tempore pro imperio populi Romani excubuisse cognitum est,*
>
> *quo ad lacum Iuturnae suum equorumque sudorem abluentis visi sunt,*
> *iunctaque fonti aedis eorum nullius hominum manu reserata patuit."*

> "It was also further found that Castor and Pollux did watch over the safety of the commonwealth, and worked hard for its good,
>
> because they were seen to wash themselves and their horses in the Lake of Juturna,
> and their temple adjoining the spring opened of its own accord, not being unlocked by the hand of any person."

Juventas (Eternal Youth, and Forgiveness)

Roman Name(s): Juventas
Greek Name(s): Ήβη, Hêbê, Hebe

Juventas is the goddess of eternal youth, the prime of life, and forgiveness. The youngest of the gods, she is often given the epithet *Ganymeda* meaning gladdening princess. She is also the cupbearer to the gods of Olympus, whom she serves ambrosia and nectar (the food and drink of the gods). The astrological symbol for Juventas and her Greek equivalent Hebe is a cup or goblet.

She is often depicted offering a cup to her father Jupiter in the form of an eagle. Eagles were symbolically connected to immortality and the folklore belief that the eagle, like the phoenix, is able to renew itself to a youthful state.

Juventas was also worshipped as a goddess of forgiveness or mercy. This association with forgiveness and mercy alongside that of eternal youth, hints at a more complex symbolic relationship between forgiveness and longer life, and its implied symmetrical opposite, containing the moral message that lack of forgiveness or mercy shortens life.

Juventas has the ability to restore youth to mortals, a power that none of the other gods appear to have, as in Ovid's Metamorphoses, where some of the gods lament the aging of their favoured mortals.

Juventas had a shrine within the inner chamber of Minerva on the Capitoline Hill. According to the Greek historian Dionysius of Halicarnassus, the sixth King of Rome, Servius Tullius, established a temple fund for Juventas which each family had to contribute to.

Latona (Motherhood, Protector of Children)

Roman Name(s): Latona
Greek Name(s): Λητώ, Leto
Etruscan Name(s): Letun

Latona is the goddess of motherhood and the protector of children. She is the mother of Diana and Apollo, fathered by Jupiter. Her Greek equivalent is Leto, the daughter of the Titans Coeus and Phoebe, and the sister of Asteria.

Based on the Greek mythology, Latona's hidden beauty caught the eye of Jupiter, who fathered their twins Diana and Apollo. Jupiter's wife Juno was furious with Jupiter for his infidelity, and ordered all lands to shun Latona, and to deny her any shelter with which to give birth.

Latona eventually managed to find shelter on the island of Delos. Diana was born first, and immediately assisted her mother in the delivery of her brother Apollo, hence Diana is also associated with childbirth. Latona was usually worshipped together with Diana and Apollo, particularly on the sacred island of Delos.

After her troubling labour on the island of Delos, Latona took her newborn infants, Diana and Apollo, over to Lycia (a region in southwestern Asia Minor) where she attempted to bathe her children and drink from a spring she had found there.

The local Lycian people tried to stop her by stirring the bottom of the spring so that mud would float up and dirty the water. Enraged over their lack of hospitality, Latona turned them all into frogs, doomed to forever swim and hop in the murky waters of the spring.

Lucifer (The Morning Star, The Light-Bringer)

Roman Name(s): Lucifer
Greek Name(s): *Φωσφόρος*, Phosphorus, *Ἑωσφόρος*, Eosphorus

The name Lucifer is most commonly associated with one of the names for the Devil in Christian theology. In the late-4th-century translation of the bible into Latin (the Vulgate), the name is uncapitalised, i.e. *lucifer*, meaning the morning star, light-bringing, or the shining one, which was originally used to refer to the planet Venus.

The ancient Greeks described the planets as wandering stars (*πλάνητες,* plánētes = wandering + *ἀστέρες,* astéres = stars), which in Latin became simply *planeta*, or *planetes*, and then planet or planets in English.

The Greek name for the planet Venus was variously given as *Φωσφόρος*, Phosphorus (light-bringer, the star of dusk), or *Ἑωσφόρος*, Eosphorus (dawn-bringer, god of the dawn star sometimes Hesperus). They were originally regarded as two distinct deities, but they were both later combined into one.

In some versions of mythology, Lucifer is the son of Aurora, the goddess of the Dawn (known as Eos in the Greek tradition). According to Hesiod, his father is Astraeus, the Titan god of the stars, planets, and astrology.

Lucifer is commonly depicted in pottery of the ancient world as a youthful man, either in the form of a bust surrounded by the shining orb of his star, or as a winged god holding a torch and crowned with a shining circle of light.

Luna (The Moon)

Roman Name(s): Luna
Greek Name(s): Σεληνη, Selênê, Selene
Etruscan Name(s): Losna, Tiur

Luna is the goddess of the moon. She is the sister of Sol (the god of the sun), and Aurora (the goddess of the dawn). She drives her moon chariot across the heavens each night.

Luna is often depicted with a crescent moon above her head, a chariot, a torch, and a billowing cloak. Her day of the week is Monday, which the Romans called Lunae Dies (moon day).

She is frequently associated and identified with Diana and Trivia who are also considered to be strongly associated with the moon. Diana and Trivia are also considered to be goddesses of the moon themselves.

Luna is sometimes associated with childbirth, due to the ancient tradition of tracking women's fertility by the cycles of the moon, and the belief that during the full moon women had the easiest of labours giving birth, this was instrumental in her being identified with Diana.

Luna is one of the *Dii Selecti* (the chosen gods), a list of the twenty principal gods of Roman religion according to Varro (recorded by Augustine of Hippo in his work De Civitate Dei or The City of God in the 5th century CE).

According to Varro, who was of Sabine origin, Luna was originally worshipped by the Sabines in the Central *Apennine* Mountains before being adopted by the Romans.

Magna Mater (Great Mother of the Mountains)

Roman Name(s): Magna Mater
Greek Name(s): *Κυβηλη*, Kybêlê, Cybele

Magna Mater (the Great Mother) is the Roman version of an ancient goddess of Phrygian origin, *Matar Kubileya* or *Kubeleya* = mother of the mountain.

She was originaly worshipped in the mountains of central and western Anatolia or Asia Minor as a mountain mother goddess, possibly the only known goddess in the region, or certainly the most important, and possibly a national deity.

The *Matar* part of her name became Magna Mater for the Romans, and the Greeks took the second half of her name *Kubileya* as Cybele.

The astrological symbol for Magna Mater or her Greek equivalent Cybele represents a mountain.

She may have evolved from the traditional seated full figured fertility goddess found at Çatalhöyük in Anatolia dated to around the 6th millennium BCE.

The Greeks in Anatolia adopted and adapted her Phrygian cult and spread it to mainland Greece in around the 6th century BCE.

She became partly associated with Terra Mater (the goddess of the earth), Ops (the Queen of the gods), and Ceres (the goddess of the harvest).

For some ancient cults she remained something of a foreign and exotic mystery goddess associated with mountains, whose rites involved her traditionally arriving in a lion drawn chariot, accompanied by wild music and an ecstatic and disorderly following.

Magna Mater was invoked as a key religious ally in the second war against Carthage from 218 to 201 BCE. Roman mythographers interpreted Cybele as a Trojan goddess, since she had been worshipped in the broader Anatolian cultural sphere, of which Troy was a part.

Cybele became an ancestral goddess of the Roman people by way of the Trojan prince Aeneas who was the first true hero of Rome. As Rome came to dominate the Mediterranean, Romanised forms of Magna Mater's cults spread throughout the Roman Empire.

As a protector of cities or city states, she was sometimes shown wearing a mural crown representing the walls of the city. Beyond this role however, there have been debates and disputes as to the overall meaning and morality of her cults, debates which have continued among scholars to this day.

Her images and iconography in funerary contexts, and the importance of the name Matar (mother) suggest that she is a mediator between the boundaries of the known and unknown, the civilised and the wild, the worlds of the living and the dead.

Mare (The Primordial Sea)

Roman Name(s): Mare
Greek Name(s): Θαλασσα, Thalassa, Thalatta

Mare is the goddess or divine personification of the sea. According to Hyginus, she is the offspring of Aether (god of the bright upper-heaven) and Dies (goddess of the day). As the daughter of Aether, she is therefore the sister of Terra Mater (goddess of the Earth) and Caelus (god of the sky). Her Greek equivalent is Thalassa.

According to Hyginus in the preface of his Fabluae, Mare (The Sea) and Pontus (The Sea) together produced all of the fish and other sea creatures.

As amorphous elemental deities representing the sea, Mare and Pontus were later ruled over by the anthropomorphic gods Neptune and Salacia.

Several of Aesop's fables involve Mare or Thalassa as the personification of the sea. Fable no. 276 reads:

A farmer saw a ship and her crew about to sink into the sea as the ship's prow disappeared beneath the curl of a wave. The farmer said, "O sea, it would have been better if no one had ever set sail on you! You are a pitiless element of nature and an enemy to mankind". When she heard this, Thalassa (the Sea) took on the shape of a woman and said in reply, "Do not spread such evil stories about me! I am not the cause of any of these things that happen to you; the Winds (Venti) to which I am exposed are the cause of them all. If you look at me when the Winds are gone, and sail upon me then, you will admit that I am even more gentle than that dry land of yours".

Mars (War, Courage, Bravery, and Destruction)

Roman Name(s): Mars
Greek Name(s): Άρης, Arês, Ares
Etruscan Name(s): Laran

Mars is the god of war who symbolises bravery and courage in war, and the physical valour necessary for success in battle. The darker side to Mars however, is that he also symbolises bloodlust, brutality, and the destructive chaos of war, something phenomenally difficult to contain once unleashed. Mars was born of Jupiter and Juno.

The ancient Romans' relationship with Mars was somewhat complex because of these two different sides. His savagery and beastliness was the opposite of what the ancient Romans aspired to. In times of war however, the unleashing of such qualities alongside bravery and valour is perhaps a calculated risk, a tactical necessity, and a necessary evil when all else has failed.

The astrological symbols for Mars or his Greek equivalent Ares represent a shield and a spear. In the 1750s the Swedish biologist Carl Linnaeus introduced the convention of using this symbol to represent the male sex.

When Vulcan discovered that his wife Venus was having an affair with Mars, he trapped them both in a net and exposed them to the ridicule of the other gods, a narrative which symbolically checks Mars as capable of being outwitted. Mars's affair with Venus produced the twin personifications of fear Metus & Pavor, and contrastingly the goddess Concordia (Condord) whom the Greeks knew as Harmonia (Harmony).

As the Roman world expanded, Mars evolved from an agricultural protector to the protector of the Roman nation, becoming indistinguishable with the Greek Ares and ultimately the same god.

Mars is one of the *Dii Selecti* (the chosen gods), a list of the twenty principal gods of Roman religion according to Varro (recorded by Augustine of Hippo in his work De Civitate Dei or The City of God in the 5th century CE).

Mars is also one of the major *Dii Flaminales*, gods who were cultivated by flamines, special priests who were assigned to the official cults during the Roman Republic.

Cities across the Roman and Greek world held festivals to keep Mars as a protector, and to ask that his savagery and brutality be kept facing outwards towards any would-be enemies, rather than inwards towards self destruction.

"Under conditions of peace the warlike man attacks himself".

F.W. Nietzsche, Beyond Good and Evil (IV. 76.)

Mercury (The Divine Messenger)

Roman Name(s): Mercurius, Mercury
Greek Name(s): Ἑρμῆς, Hermês, Hermes
Etruscan Name(s): Turms

Mercury is the god of athletes, boundaries, commerce, cunning, hospitality, language, merchants, messages, oratory, roads, shepherds, speed, thieves, travellers, and wit.

He is the son of Jupiter and Maia (one of the Pleiades).

He also serves as a divine messenger for his father Jupiter.

His winged sandals allow him to move quickly and freely between the worlds of the mortal and the divine. He also plays the role of a guide who transfers souls to the afterlife.

He is depicted holding a winged staff entwined with two snakes called a caduceus. The astrological symbol for Mercury and his Greek equivalent Hermes is a representation of this caduceus, a powerful symbol that is documented among the Babylonians as far back as 3500 BCE. The caduceus was also used in depictions of the Mesopotamian god Ningishzida, who like Mercury is a mediator between humans and the divine.

Mercury is sometimes depicted wearing a *petasus*, a type of sun hat which was representative of rural peoples. Sometimes this hat was winged, and later the wings rose directly from his head, influenced by the equivalent Etruscan god Turms.

From 800 BCE to around 480 BCE he was depicted as an older bearded man dressed as a traveller, herald, or shepherd. This image remained on the boundary markers, roadside markers, and votive offerings which were called *Mercuriae*, pillar-like in shape with the head of Mercury at the top. These *Mercuriae* later appeared as grave monuments, symbolising Mercury's role as a transporter of souls to the Underworld. He was later depicted as a young athletic and clean-shaven man.

In Ptolemaic Egypt, the dual worship of Thoth and Mercury (Hermes) led to Mercury becoming associated with translation and interpretation, or more generally a god of knowledge and learning. In the temple at Esna on the west bank of the Nile the epithet 'Thoth the great, the great, the great' was applied to Mercury (Hermes) at around 172 BCE. This led to Mercury being referred to as *Mercurius Trismegistus* (the thrice-greatest Mercury). Mercury was also known as *Mercurius ter Maximus* (Mercury the three times greatest) and was said to be the inspiration for Mercurianism or Mercurian Philosophy, with core principles such as the importance of communication, the power of the mind, the interconnectedness of all things, and the importance of adaptability.

Mercury is one of the *Dii Selecti* (the chosen gods), a list of the twenty principal gods of Roman religion according to Varro (recorded by Augustine of Hippo in his work De Civitate Dei or The City of God in the 5th century CE).

Minerva (Wisdom, Strategy, Battle, and Crafts)

Roman Name(s): Minerva
Greek Name(s): *Αθηνη*, Athênê, Athena
Etruscan Name(s): Menrva

Minerva is the goddess of wisdom, justice, law, victory, and the sponsor of the arts, trade, and strategy. She is also a goddess of warfare with an emphasis on strategic warfare rather than the blind ugly violence of gods such as Mars. In times of peace Minerva represents creativity, weaving, pottery, and handicraft in general.

She is commonly depicted wearing a shield and a war helmet, carrying a spear, and accompanied by her owl which represents wisdom.

Minerva's father is Jupiter, and her mother is Metis, a goddess of wisdom. Metis was an advisor to Jupiter and became his first wife. She was both a threat to him and indispensably helpful to him.

She had helped him to free his siblings from their father Saturn's stomach by giving him an emetic, causing him to vomit them all back out.

After Jupiter had impregnated Metis, he immediately feared the consequences, especially when it was foretold that Metis would give birth to a daughters wiser than the mother, and then give birth to a son more powerful than the father who would overthrow him and become ruler of the cosmos in his place.

Jupiter had overthrown his father Saturn, who had overthrown his father Caelus, and Jupiter feared that he in turn would be overthrown by his sown offspring. In an attempt to prevent Metis from giving birth, Jupiter tricked Metis into turning herself into a fly, and then promptly swallowed her. Inside Jupiter, Metis crafted armour, a spear, and a shield for Minerva and raised her inside Jupiter's mind, where Metis remained and continued to be a source of Jupiter's wisdom.

Eventually Minerva used her spear and shield, banging them together to make a loud noise, giving Jupiter an awful headache. When this headache became unbearable, Jupiter had Vulcan cut his head open. Minerva burst out of Jupiter's head fully grown, fully clothed, and fully armed, and was then made the goddess of wisdom, warfare, and crafts.

Minerva's Greek counterpart is Athena, and in Egyptian mythology she is comparable to Neith, in Phoenician mythology as Anat, and Zoroastrian mythology as Anahita. The Astrological symbol for Minerva or Athena is based on the head of a spear.

Minerva is one of the *Dii Selecti* (the chosen gods), a list of the twenty principal gods of Roman religion according to Varro (recorded by Augustine of Hippo in his work De Civitate Dei or The City of God in the 5th century CE).

According to Varro, who was of Sabine origin, Minerva was originally worshipped by the Sabines in the Central Apennine Mountains before being adopted by the Romans.

Mithras (The Persian, Light, Truth, and Oaths)

Mithras Plaque, Author's Collection

Roman Name(s): Mithras, Mithra, Mitra

Mithras is the Roman version of the Indo-Iranian god Mithra, a god of light, truth, oaths and contracts, believed to have been worshipped in Persia as early as the second millennium BCE.

The Romans drew parallels between gods from other cultures and their own by comparing their characteristics. The Romans also prayed to the gods of their enemies, hoping to tip the balance in their favour, and while they had their own well established state religion, their territorial expansion brought them into contact with other cults and deities, which they absorbed and a their own traditions.

In astrology, the planets were named from the Olympian gods, and when Roman scholars studied Greek astrology, they used the Latin names instead.

A common image in Mithraism is the Tauroctony, which represents Mithras slaying the sacred bull, which brought about the creation of the cosmos. Modern scholars have drawn parallels with elements in the Tauroctony and their corresponding constellations, notably that the constellation of Perseus (The Persian) is Mithras, because he is wearing a Phrygian cap, an item of clothing that the Roman world would have recognised as having been something eastern, something Persian.

Taurus is The Bull, Canis Major is The Dog, Gemini (Castor and Pollux) are The Torch Bearers, Hydra is The Snake, Corvus is The Crow, Crater is The Goblet, and Leo is the Small Lion. When observing the celestial equator, it was possible to see the constellation of Perseus (The Persian, Mithras) rising up over The Bull (Taurus), and then both constellations dipping below the celestial equator and out of sight. This phenomenon was mythologised as Mithras slaying the bull.

Mithraism was also very popular with the Roman Army, because of its structure, which consisted of grades of initiation all having their own symbols and meanings. This hierarchical structure was compatible with the hierarchy of Roman society. With the roman state religion tolerating the worship of multiple deities, as long as roman subjects were loyal to Rome, and saw themselves as citizens of Rome first.

In the later Roman Empire the 25th December was an important date for celebrating *Dies Natlis Solis Invicti* (The day of the birth of the unconquerable sun), and Mithras was often celebrated along with Sol Invictus, as were many other gods in the Roman pantheon.

Many of the Mithraea that are preserved today exist underneath the churches that were built on top of them. Churches built in the 5th Century A.D. were often on top of ruins of important buildings such as places of worship of other gods, such as Mithras. This is particularly true in Rome, where at least four Mithraea exist under churches.

> "If the growth of Christianity had been arrested by some mortal malady, the world would have been Mithraic"
>
> Ernest Renan, 1882

Moneta (Memory and Remembrance)

Roman Name(s): Moneta
Greek Name(s): *Μνημοσυνη*, Mnêmosynê, Mnemosyne

Moneta is the goddess of memory and remembrance, and the inventor of language and words. She represents the memorising of the stories of history, myth, and poetry before the introduction of writing.

She is the daughter of Caelus (The Sky) and Terra Mater (The Earth). Hyginus suggests that Aether may be her father instead of Caelus.

Moneta gave birth to the nine Muses who originally represented all of the liberal arts collectively, including poetry, with Jupiter as their father.

From the 5th to the 4th centuries BCE onwards, the Muses began to be recognised, identified, and assigned more specific aspects of the liberal arts individually.

By her association with the Muses, Moneta is also associated with music and poetry. Some sources identify Moneta with one of the Elder Muses or Boeotian Muses known as Mneme (literally memory).

The name Moneta comes from the word *monere*, meaning to remind, to warn, or to instruct. The name is also used as an epithet for the Roman goddess Juno (Hera), i.e. Juno Moneta.

Morpheus (The Shaper of Dreams)

Roman Name(s): Morpheus
Greek Name(s): Μορφευς, Morpheus

Morpheus is the personification of dreams, and the leader of the thousand dreams spirits known collectively as the Somnia.

His name translates as the Fashioner, or the Shaper, which comes from the ancient Greek word *morphé* or *morfí* (μορφή), meaning shape, form, or figure. He is the son of Somnus (Sleep), and Pasithea (the personification of relaxation, meditation, and hallucinations).

As well as representing sleep and dreams and leading the Somnia, Morpheus also shapes and forms the dreams of mortals, in which he has the power to appear in human guise to deliver messages from the gods. His domain is Scotus (Erebus), the Primordial darkness that encircles the world and fills the deep hollows of the earth.

Ovid is the first to name him in his narrative poem Metamorphoses as the son of Somnus:

"Morphea: non illic quisquam sollertius alter

exprimit incessus vultumque sonumque loquendi."
…
"Est etiam diversae tertius artis
Phantasos: ille in humum saxumque undamque trabemque
quaeque vacant anima, fallaciter omnia transit."

"Morpheus: there is no one other more clever than
he at expressesing the gait, the countenance, and the tone of speech."
…
"There is also a different third art
Phantasos: he into the ground and the rock and the wave and the beam
and every empty soul passes through everything by deception."

The opiate morphine gets its name from the god Morpheus. The use of opium from poppies (*papaver somniferum*) as a pain medication and a treatment of stomach complaints and other ailments dates back to ancient times, long before the ancient Greeks. The amount of active ingredients (alkaloids) in opium has always varied considerably, historically making controlled dosage notoriously difficult. In 1804 the German pharmacist Friedrich Sertürner successfully isolated these alkaloids. He hoped that by isolating the morphine and controlling the amount in each dose, the problems of overdose and addiction could be avoided. He first named it *morphium* after the god Morpheus because it had a tendency to cause sleep, and it later became known as *morphine*.

Gods and goddesses descended from Nyx, such as Morpheus, Somnus, and Mors, have long been metaphorically associated with trance, sleep, and death, and in art they have long been depicted with poppies, scattering poppies, or with poppies nearby. With the revival of classical learning, this iconography continued in paintings from the Renaissance period onwards.

Mors (Peaceful Death)

Roman Name(s): Mors, Letus, Thanatus
Greek Name(s): Θανατος, Thanatos, Thanatos
Etruscan Name(s): Leinth, Charun

Mors is the personification of death. He is often referred to but rarely appearing in person.

According to Hesiod's Theogony, he is the son of Nox (Nyx) without a father. Hyginus and Cicero both name Scotus (Erebus) as the father.

Next to his twin brother Somnus (Sleep), Mors lives in a cave in the Underworld, where day and night meet, but where no sunlight or sound enters. At the entrance to his cave there are poppies growing, along with other sleep inducing plants.

Somnus and Mors are the subject of a painting by John William Waterhouse called Sleep and His Half-Brother Death, depicting the two figures side by side. The lighter figure in the foreground is Sleep (Somnus) holding poppies in his hands, and the darker figure in the background is Death (Mors).

Gods and goddesses descended from Nyx, such as Morpheus, Somnus, and Mors, have long been metaphorically associated with trance, sleep, and death, and in art they have long been depicted with poppies, scattering poppies, or with poppies nearby. With the revival of classical learning, this iconography continued in paintings from the Renaissance period onwards.

Mors is named as one of the *Dii Inferi* (the gods below), the shadowy collective of ancient Roman deities associated with death and the Underworld.

Natura (Nature)

Roman Name(s): Natura, Primagena
Greek Name(s): Φυσις, Physis, Πρωτογενεια, Prôtogeneia

Natura is the primordial goddess of nature, the origin and order of nature.

In the Orphic tradition, she emerged at the beginning of time, and is referred to as Primagena or Protogeneia (the first born). Her Greek equivalent is Physis.

Philostratus the Younger in his Imagines (3) writes:

"ὁρᾷς δέ που καὶ τὸ περὶ τὴν πηγὴν ἄλσος φύσεως ἔργον, οἶμαι, τῆς σοφῆς: ἱκανὴ γὰρ πάντα, ὅσα βούλεται, καὶ δεῖται τέχνης οὐδέν, ἥ γε καὶ τέχναις αὐταῖς ἀρχὴ καθέστηκε."

"No doubt you see the grove around the spring, the work of wise Natura (Physis), I believe; for Natura (Physis) is sufficient for all she desires, and has no need of art; indeed it is she who is the origin of arts themselves."

In Nonnus's Dionysiaca (book 2) after a great battle between Zeus and Typhon that affects the whole cosmos, Natura (Physis) repairs the earth, returning the cosmos to its natural order:

"καὶ ταμίη κόσμοιο,
παλιγγενέος Φύσις ὕλης,
ῥηγνυμένης κενεῶνα κεχηνότα πῆξεν ἀρούρης,
νησαίους δὲ τένοντας ἀποτμηγέντας ἐναύλων
ἁρμονίης ἀλύτοιο πάλιν σφρηγίσσατο δεσμῷ.

οὐκέτι δὲ κλόνος ἦεν ἐν ἄστρασιν:

ἠέλιος γὰρ χαιτήεντα Λέοντα παρὰ σταχυώδεϊ
Κούρῃ Ζῳδιακῆς ἔστησε παραΐξαντα κελεύθου:
οὐρανίου δὲ Λέοντος ἐπισκαίροντα
προσώπῳ καρκίνον ἀντικέλευθον ἀθαλπέος
Αἰγοκερῆος ἂψ ἀνασειράζουσα διεστήριξε
Σελήνη."

"and the treasurer of the world,
Nature (Physis) the creator of matter,
closed up the emptiness in earth's broken surface,
and sealed once more with the bond of indivisible joinery those island cliffs which had been rent from their beds.
No longer was there turmoil among the stars.
For Helios replaced the maned Lion, who had moved out of the path of the Zodiac, beside the Maiden who holds the corn-ear; Selene took the crab, now crawling over the forehead of the heavenly Lion, and drew him back opposite cold Capricorn, and fixt him there."

Necessitas (Necessity, Compulsion, Inevitability)

Roman Name(s): Necessitas
Greek Name(s): *Αναγκη*, Anankê, Ananke

Necessitas is the Primordial personification of necessity, compulsion, and inevitability, both in terms of the beginning of creation, and in terms of the rotation of the heavens driving time and therefore driving destiny forward unstoppably.

In the Orphic tradition she emerged self-formed at the beginning of creation, initially envisaged as a serpentine figure with outstretched arms that encompassed the cosmos. With her consort Chronos (Time), also in serpentine form, they coiled themselves around the Cosmic Egg or World Egg, causing it to split apart. Out of this egg hatched Protogonus the god of creation, who created the earth, the sea, and the sky. After their part in the act of creation, Chronos and Necessitas then circled the cosmos, driving the rotation of the heavens and the eternal passage of time.

Necessitas is sometimes depicted as holding a spindle, a symbol of the entwining and spinning of fate and destiny.

Plato, in his Republic, mentions the Parcae (the Moirai) as the daughters of Necessitas, who are also depicted as spinning, measuring, and cutting the threads of fate.

Her Greek equivalent is Ananke, and she is also known as Adrastia meaning inescapable and also Tecmor meaning purpose, end, goal.

Orphic Fragment 54 suggests alternatively that Necessitas (Ananke) was born of Hydros (The Primordial Waters) and Terra Mater (Mother Earth).

Neptune (The Sea)

Roman Name(s): Neptunus, Neptune
Greek Name(s): Ποσειδων, Poseidôn, Poseidon
Etruscan Name(s): Nethuns

Neptune is the Olympian god of the sea, earthquakes, floods, droughts, and also horses. He is depicted as an old man holding a trident (a fisherman's spear, tri = three + dent = tooth). His Greek equivalent is Poseidon. At birth Neptune was swallowed whole by his father Saturn along with his siblings, but Jupiter later gained the assistance of Metis who fed Saturn with a magical elixir causing Saturn to vomit back up Neptune and his siblings.

Neptune's trident was crafted for him with magical powers by the Cyclopes (the one-eyed giants: Brontes, Stereops, and Arges) a weapon with which he is famously associated with. Poseidon claimed joint rulership over the cosmos with his brothers Jupiter and Pluto. They drew lots to decide which of the realms they would rule. Jupiter had the sky, Neptune had the sea, and Pluto had the Underworld.

Neptune seduced many nymphs and mortal woman often in the guise of an animal, or flowing water. Some of his most famous conquests were the Gorgon Medusa, Tyro, Amymone, and Aithra mother of the hero Theseus. In one myth Neptune entered a contest with the goddess Minerva for dominion over Athens and produced the very first horse as a gift. But the king refused him the prize and in anger Neptune afflicted the land with drought.

Neptune is one of the *Dii Selecti* (the chosen gods), a list of the twenty principal gods of Roman religion according to Varro (recorded by Augustine of Hippo in his work De Civitate Dei or The City of God in the 5th century CE).

Nox (The Night)

Roman Name(s): Nox
Greek Name(s): *Nuξ*, Nyx

Nox is the personification of the night, who emerged at the dawn of creation. Her Greek equivalent is Nyx.

She is the daughter of Chaos (The Void) and the sister of Scotus (Erebus, The Darkness).

According to Hesiod, Nox and Scotus produced Aether (The Bright Upper-Heavens), and Dies (The Day).

In the Orphic tradition Nox is the daughter and consort of Protogonus (The Creator).

On her own, Nox produced a number of dark spirits including Fatum (Doom, Destiny), The Tenebrae (Destruction, Death), Mors (Peaceful Death), Somnia (Sleep), the Somnia (Dream-Spirits), the Parcae (The Three Fates), Invidia (Retribution), Discordia (Strife).

Every evening Nox draws her veil of dark mists across the sky, obscuring the light of Aether. This dark veil is composed of the darkness of Scotus, which she either wears around her and then unfurls across the sky, or draws across the sky with a chariot.

Her opposite is her daughter Dies (The Day) who scatters the mists of night each dawn, and thus Nox and Dies pass each other each day at the entrance to their dwelling in the Underworld.

One myth states that even Jupiter was afraid of Nox, because she was much older and more powerful than him. When Jupiter was furious with Somnus for having made him fall asleep at Juno's request, Somnus fled to his mother Nox for protection, and Jupiter did not dare to pursue him any further for fear of upsetting or angering Nox.

In ancient art Nox is depicted as a winged goddess or a charioteer, crowned by a circle of dark mists, wearing a large black cloak or black robes. In 1883 the French painter William-Adolphe Bouguereau painted La Nuit, a then modern interpretation of Nox. In his painting, Nox has her black robe, and is also surrounded by four owls, which are commonly known as creatures of the night.

Nox and her descendents, such as Morpheus, Somnia, and Mors, have long been metaphorically associated with trance, sleep, and death, and in art they have long been depicted with poppies, scattering poppies, or with poppies nearby.

With the revival of classical learning, this iconography continued in paintings from the Renaissance period onwards. The Pre-Raphaelite influenced painting Night and Sleep by Evelyn de Morgan in 1878 features Nox and Somnus figuratively travelling across the sky from east to west (left to right), scattering poppies as they go.

Ops (Queen of the Heavens)

Roman Name(s): Magna Mater, Ops, Opis
Greek Name(s): *Ρεια*, *Ρεα*, Rheia, Rhea

Ops is a queen of the the heavens, and the mother of the eldest Olympian gods (Vesta, Ceres, Juno, Neptune, Pluto, and Jupiter). Her Greek equivalent is Rhea, a name which means flow or ease, and as such she represents the eternal flow of time and generations, and comfort and ease. She was also identified with the goddess Magna Mater (Great Mother) along with the mother goddess Cybele. Like the mother goddess Cybele, she is often depicted with lions.

As the mother of the gods, Ops symbolises and represents motherhood and fertility. She is the daughter of Caelus (The Sky) and Terra Mater (The Earth), and the wife of Saturn (Time).

Ops's brother and husband Saturn feared being overthrown by his offspring, and so he swallowed each of their children as they were born. When Ops bore the sixth and final child Jupiter, she had him spirited him away to Crete under the protection of the nymph Amalthea to be raised in hiding.

Ops appointed three, five, or nine rustic spirits called the Curetes or the Dactyli to guard Jupiter in a cave on Mount Ida. They drowned out the infant cries of Jupiter with dancing and clashing their shields with spears. Ops then tricked Saturn into swallowing a rock wrapped in swaddling bands instead, believing it to be Jupiter. Jupiter was assisted by Metis who gave Saturn an emetic, making him vomit back up the children he had swallowed. Jupiter eventually overthrew his father Saturn.

According to Varro, who was of Sabine origin, Ops was originally worshipped by the Sabines in the Central Apennine Mountains before being adopted by the Romans.

The Parcae (The Three Fates)

Roman Name(s): Parcae, Fatae
Greek Name(s): *Μοιρα*, *Μοιραι*, Moira, Moirai

The Parcae are the three personifications of fate, often referred to as The Fates. They decide the fate and destiny of every human life. The Greeks knew them as the Moirai.

Nona is the youngest of the fates known as the spinner. She spins the thread of each human life on her spindle, and also decides when each person is born. Her Greek equivalent is Clotho.

Decima is the middle of the fates known as the dispenser of lots. She measures the thread of each human life as it leaves Nona's spindle. She decides how long each thread of life will be. Her Greek equivalent is Lachesis.

Morta is the elder of the fates. She is known as the inflexible one or she who cannot be turned, and she chooses the manner of death and the ending of each human life by cutting their threads. Her Greek equivalent is Atropos. Also known as Parca Maurtia, she is is named as one of the *Dii Inferi* (the gods below), the shadowy collective of ancient Roman deities associated with death and the Underworld.

There are many different versions or accounts of their parentage, among them are Jupiter and Themis, or Scotus and Nox, etc. Plato in his Republic suggests that they are the daughters of Necessitas (Necessity).

Parcae is the plural of Parca, which in Latin means a spare, sparing, frugal, or thrifty.

Pax (Peace)

Roman Name(s): Pax
Greek Name(s): *Εἰρήνη*, Eirene

Pax is the goddess and personification of peace. She is the daughter of Jupiter and Justitia, and her Greek equivalent is Eirene. She is commonly depicted holding out olive branches as a peace offering, also with a caduceus (a winged staff), a cornucopia (a horn of plenty), corn, and a sceptre.

The worship of Pax was organised and made popular during the rule of the first Roman Emperor, Gaius Julius Caesar Augustus, also known as Augustus or Octavian (27 BCE to 14 CE).

The worship of Pax was an important way of symbolically stabilising the empire after the years of turmoil and civil war of the late Roman Republic.

An altar of peace in honour of the goddess Pax was commissioned and built on the Campus Martius to honour the return of Augustus to Rome after three years in Hispania and Gaul. The altar was initially known as the Ara Pacis Augustae (The Altar of Augustan Peace), but it was later shortened to Ara Pacis (The Altar of Peace). The emperor Vespasian built a temple in her honour called the Templum Pacis (The Temple of Peace). A festival was held for her on the 30th day of January.

The peace that followed lasted roughly 200 years and was identified as a golden age of increased and sustained Roman imperialism, relative peace and order, prosperous stability, and regional expansion. It was known as *Pax Romana* (Roman Peace) and lasted until the death of Marcus Aurelius, the last of the so-called Five Good Emperors, in 180 CE.

Pluto, Orcus, and Dis Pater (The Underworld)

Roman Name(s): Dis Pater, Orcus, Pluto
Greek Name(s): Άιδης, Haidês, Hades
Etruscan Name(s): Aita

Pluto is the god of the dead, and the king of the Underworld, the unseen realm to which the souls of the dead go upon leaving the world.

He presides over funeral rites and defends the right of the dead to due burial.

He is depicted holding a bident, a helm or cap of invisibility, and with Cerberus the dog standing by his side (some say that Cerberus has three heads, some say fifty).

Pluto claimed joint rulership over the cosmos with his brothers Jupiter and Neptune.

They drew lots to decide which of the realms they would rule.

Jupiter had the sky, Neptune had the sea, and Pluto had the Underworld, with which his name became synonymous.

He was originally known as Orcus or Dis Pater, similar to the Etruscan god Aite. He is named as one of the *Dii Inferi* (the gods below), the shadowy collective of ancient Roman deities associated with death and the Underworld.

These various names were merged into Pluto, which was a latinisation of Plouton meaning the rich one, a euphemistic title that the Greeks gave to Hades out of a superstitious aversion to mentioning his actual name.

Pluto's earlier name Orcus is one of the *Dii Selecti* (the chosen gods), a list of the twenty principal gods of Roman religion according to author Varro (recorded by Augustine of Hippo in his work De Civitate Dei or The City of God in the 5th century CE).

Pluto abducted Proserpina and made her his wife and Queen of the Underworld. Proserpina's mother Ceres was devastated by this abduction and asserted that the earth would be barren until she saw her daughter again.

Jupiter proposed a compromise whereby Proserpina would have her time divided between the underworld and the earth and Mount Olympus, to which Pluto agreed.

Proserpina's return from the Underworld to the earth every year coincides with the retreat of the barren winter and the arrival of spring and the return of vegetation and grain crops.

Pomona (Abundance, Fruit Trees)

Roman Name(s): Pomona

Pomona is the goddess of plenty, fruitful abundance, and fruit trees. She is also described as a wood nymph, a female personification or maiden of nature tied to a specific place, land, or tree. She is not associated with the harvest of fruits as such, but more with the flourishing of the fruit trees.

She does not have a clear counterpart or equivalent in Greek mythology, although the fruit goddess Opora (Ὀπώρα), a Greek minor goddess connected to fruit, the harvest, and wine harvest, could be seen as her equivalent. She is also associated with the goddess Ceres (known as Demeter in the Greek tradition).

According to Ovid, Pomona scorned the love of the woodland gods Silvanus and Picus, but was seduced by and married Vertumnus, the god of seasonal changes. Pomona and Vertumnus are both celebrated in the festival of Vertumnalia on the 13th day of August.

A sacred grove in honour of Pomona called the Pomonal is located near the ancient Roman port of Ostia.

Pomona is often depicted with a pruning knife, a traditional multi-purpose agricultural hand tool, also known as a billhook, with a short curved blade and a wooden handle, the use of which dates back at least as far as the Bronze Age. She is also depicted with a cornucopia (a horn of plenty), or holding a platter of fruit.

Pomona is one of the minor *Dii Flaminales*, gods who were cultivated by flamines (*flamen Pomonalis*), special priests who were assigned to the official cults during the Roman Republic.

Proserpina (The Underworld and Spring Growth)

Roman Name(s): Proserpina
Greek Name(s): *Περσεφονη*, Persephonê, Persephone
Etruscan Name(s): Persipnei

Proserpina is the goddess and queen of the underworld, and the goddess of spring growth.

She is sometimes depicted as a young goddess holding sheafs of grain and a flaming torch.

Proserpina is the daughter of Jupiter (the god of the sky and ruler of Olympus) and Ceres (the goddess of agriculture).

Proserpina was in a flowery meadow when she was abducted by Pluto and taken down to the Underworld to be his wife.

Her mother Ceres frantically searched all over the world for her, assisted by Trivia with her torches.

When Ceres finally learned that Proserpina had been taken to the Underworld by Pluto to be his wife, she was devastated.

When Ceres further learned that Jupiter (Proserpina's own father) had given Pluto his approval for the abduction, Ceres was furious.

She immediately stopped her duties as the goddess of agriculture and refused to allow the earth to bear fruit until her daughter was returned. The earth turned barren, and all life on earth was at risk of starvation.

Jupiter finally agreed to Ceres's demand for Proserpina's return, but because Proserpina had eaten a handful of pomegranate seeds from the Underworld she was then bound to the Underworld. She was forced to spend part of the year in the Underworld, and the rest of the year up on the earth.

Her yearly return to the earth is marked by the flowering of the meadows and the growth of spring. Her return to the Underworld is marked by the dying down of plants, a pause in growth, and the onset of winter.

According to the Orphic tradition, Proserpina and Pluto produced the Dirae, also known as The Furies, three goddesses of vengeance and retribution who punish people for their crimes. There are various names given to the the three Dirae, including Tisiphone, Megaria, and Alecto.

In the Eleusinian Mysteries, Proserpina's return from the Underworld is seen as a symbol of resurrection and immortality.

Proserpina is named as one of the *Dii Inferi* (the gods below), the shadowy collective of ancient Roman deities associated with death and the Underworld.

Protogonus (The Creator)

Roman Name(s): Protogonus, Protogenus
Greek Name(s): Φανης, Phanês, Phanes

In the Orphic tradition, Protogonus is the Primordial god of creation. He is the generator of life, and the driving force behind reproduction in the early cosmos.

At the dawn of creation, the Cosmic Egg or World Egg existed in the Aether (Bright Upper-Heaven). Necessitas (Necessity) and Chronos (Time) in their serpent form entwined themselves around the Cosmic Egg or World Egg and caused it to break open.

Protogonus hatched forth from the egg along with a chaotic mix of primordial matter, and Protogonus then used the primordial matter to create the earth, the sea, and the sky.

After all creation was complete, Protogonus handed over his sceptre to his daughter Nox (The Night). Nox then handed the sceptre to her son Caelus (The Sky). The sceptre was then seized from Caelus by Saturn (Time), and then from Saturn by Jupiter, the ultimate ruler of the Cosmos. Some accounts suggest that Jupiter devoured Protogonus in order to absorb his power and then redistribute it among the new generation of gods known as the Olympians.

The Orphics saw Protogonus as similar to the Primordial personification of desire Eros, as described in Hesiod's Theogony.

Protogonus is described as a beautiful golden-winged hermaphroditic deity entwined by a serpent. The name Protogonus or Protogenus means first born, similar to the Greek Protogenoi.

Querella (Mockery, Satire, and Criticism)

Roman Name(s): Querella, Momus
Greek Name(s): *Μωμος*, Mômos, Momus

Querella is the personification of mockery, satire, blame, ridicule, scorn, complaint, and harsh criticism. His Greek equivalent is Momus.

He is an important part of Greek and Roman culture as a symbol of that which exposes vices, follies, abuses, and shortcomings to ridicule.

In a civilised society this mockery and satire (and the freedom to practice it) is prized as a form of constructive social criticism, whereby individuals, corporations, governments, or society itself can be shamed into improvement.

Querella embodies the duality of harsh and unfair criticism on one hand, and holding power to account, or talking truth to power on the other hand.

Freedom comes with responsibility, and actions come with consequences, and so the cautionary tale is that Querella was expelled from the heavens by Jupiter for ridiculing the gods.

As a spirit of criticism, Querella is also associated with fault-finding. Plato in his Republic describes the idea of something so perfect that even "Momus (Querella) himself could not find fault with it".

The opposite of Querella or Momus is Eupheme (the goddess of Praise and Acclaim).

Roma (The Roman State)

Roman Name(s): Roma, Dea Roma

Roma is the goddess who personifies the city of Rome, and more generally, the Roman state. She was created and promoted to represent Rome's ideas about itself, and to justify its rule.

Roma was portrayed on coins, sculptures, buildings, and at official games and festivals. Images of Roma had elements in common with other goddesses such as Minerva and Fortuna, as the mother of a fierce warrior like people, and as a protector of the city state.

As the Roman Empire expanded, depictions of the goddess Roma evolved from a fierce warrior with a helmet and weapons, to a calm advisor and protector of ruling emperors. The emperor Hadrian built a temple dedicated to Roma called *Roma Aeterna* (Eternal Rome), emphasising the sacred, universal, and eternal nature of the empire.

In Rome's eastern provinces, Roma was often depicted wearing a mural crown (a crown that represented the walls of the city). Her image was rarely found in a domestic context alongside more personal and private worship of gods, but was favoured in formal and official contexts, including those of Imperial representatives abroad.

Her depiction as seated on a throne, wearing a helmet, and holding a shield and spear, was largely influential in the depiction of Britannia, the personification of Britain, particularly in the English Renaissance and Early Modern period onwards.

Salacia (The Depths of the Ocean)

Roman Name(s): Salacia
Greek Name(s): *Ἀμφιτρίτη*, Amphitrite

Salacia is the goddess of the sea, salt water, and the depths of the ocean. She is the wife of Neptune, the god of the sea, and together they produced Triton whose body was half man and half fish. Salacia's Greek equivalent is Amphitrite.

She is commonly depicted as a beautiful nymph, sometimes crowned with seaweed, seated beside Neptune, or riding in a pearl shell chariot drawn by dolphins, sea-horses, or other creatures of the deep.

Salacia is the personification of the calm and sunlit aspect of the sea. Derived from Latin *sal*, meaning salt, the name Salacia denotes the wide, open sea, and is sometimes literally translated as the salty one.

The god Neptune wanted to marry Salacia, but she was in great awe of her distinguished suitor, and to preserve her virginity, with grace and celerity she managed to glide out of his sight, and hid from him in the Atlantic Ocean. The grieving Neptune sent a dolphin to look for her and persuade the fair nymph to return and share his throne. Salacia agreed to marry Neptune and the King of the Deep was so overjoyed at these good tidings that the dolphin was awarded a place in the heavens, where he now forms a well known constellation Delphinus.

Salacia's name was given to that of the large trans-Neptunian object, 120347 Salacia, in the Kuiper belt. It also has a moon called Actaea, named after one of the nereids (sea nymphs).

Salus (Health, Healing, and Hygiene)

Roman Name(s): Salus, Valetudo
Greek Name(s): Ὑγεια, Hygeia, Hygieia

Salus is the goddess of good health, cleanliness, and sanitation. Her name means safety, salvation, or welfare. She has also been known as Valetudo, literally meaning good health. Her Greek equivalent Hygieia is where the English word hygiene comes from. She is one of the Asclepiades (children of Asclepius). She has four sisters: Panacea (universal remedy), Iaso (recuperation), Aceso (healing), and Aegle (good health). Their mother is Epione (the goddess of soothing pain).

Salus is often depicted holding a large serpent in her arms and a small bowl in her hand called a *patera* or a *phiale* (a shallow dish used in religious ceremonies), which she uses to feed the serpent.

The astrological symbols for Salus and her Greek counterpart Hygieia is a caduceus (a staff entwined with two snakes), a staff entwined with one snake, a snake and a star, or a bowl entwined by a snake.

The worship of Salus is closely associated with the cult of Asclepius, located in healing temples called Asclepieia across the Greek and Roman world. While Asclepius is more directly associated with healing, Salus is associated with the prevention of sickness and the continuation of good health.

Devotees would attend the temples seeking spiritual and physical healing, and some would sleep in the temple with the expectation that they would be visited by Asclepius or one of his children in their dream, which would be reported to a priest who would interpret the dream and prescribe a cure.

According to Varro, who was of Sabine origin, Salus was originally worshipped by the Sabines in the Central Apennine Mountains before being adopted by the Romans.

Saturn (Time and the Harvest)

Roman Name(s): Saturn, Saturnus
Greek Name(s): *Κρονος*, Kronos, Cronus
Etruscan Name(s): Satre

Saturn is a god of the harvest and of time, particularly when time is viewed as a destructive all-devouring force. He is often depicted with a harpe (a scythe or a sickle).

Saturn conspired with his brothers against their father Caelus, laying an ambush for him as he descended to Terra Mater in order to lay with her. They waited at the four corners of the world and seized hold of Caelus, and held him down while Saturn, who waited in the centre, castrated Caelus with the stone sickle that Terra Mater had made especially, and then threw his severed genitals into the sea.

Saturn feared being overthrown by his offspring, and so he swallowed each of them as they were born. When Ops bore the sixth and final child Jupiter, she spirited him away and hid him in Crete, tricking Saturn into swallowing a rock wrapped in swaddling bands instead. Jupiter was assisted by Metis who gave Saturn an emetic, making him vomit back up the children he had swallowed. Jupiter eventually overthrew his father Saturn.

The astrological symbol for Saturn evolved from the first two letters of the name of his Greek equivalent Cronus *κρ* (khr or cr) with the cross being added in the 16th century. Cronus (*Κρόνος*) is most frequently conflated or identified with Chronos (*Χρόνος*) due to the similarity of their names and their association with time, however the former represents linear time (past, present, future), and the latter represents cycles of time (months, years, ages, generations). Chronos means time, whereas Cronus is possibly from the ancient Greek word *krainō* (κραίνω) meaning to rule or to command, perhaps because he was the ruler of the Titans. Both gods were combined and identified with Saturn as early as the 3rd century BCE, when writers like Andronicus referred to Jupiter (Zeus) as the son of Saturn. Plutarch (On Isis and Osiris, 2.64) states that the Greeks believed Cronus was an allegorical name for Chronos, and Saturn is so called because he is filled (*saturatur*) with years.

The Romans celebrated Saturn during the festival of Saturnalia which was held on the 17th December of the Julian Calendar. By the 1st century BCE the festivities had expanded from 1 day to 7 days. It was a time of feasting, role reversals, free speech, gift giving, and revelry. A sacrifice was made to Saturn at the Temple of Saturn in the Roman Forum. The planet Saturn and the day of the week Saturday (Saturni Dies, Saturn's Day) are named after him.

Saturn is one of the *Dii Selecti* (the chosen gods), a list of the twenty principal gods of Roman religion according to Varro (recorded by Augustine of Hippo in his work De Civitate Dei or The City of God in the 5th century CE). According to Varro, who was of Sabine origin, Saturn was originally worshipped by the Sabines in the Central *Apennine* Mountains before being adopted by the Romans.

Scotus (The Darkness)

Roman Name(s): Scotus, Erebus
Greek Name(s): *Ερεβος*, Erebos, Erebus

Scotus is the personification of the darkness whose mists encircle the world and fill the deep hollows of the earth. In the evening Scotus's wife Nox (The Night) draws her dark veil composed of Scotus's darkness across the sky, obscuring Aether (The Bright Heavens) from the earth and bringing about the night. In the morning Scotus's daughter Dies (The Day) disperses the mists of the night and reveals the shining blue Aether of the day. Scotus is also used as a synonym for the Underworld as a realm of darkness.

Hesiod suggests that Scotus was born of Chaos with no father. The Orphic tradition however lists Chronos (Time) & Necessitas (Necessity) as the parents of Scotus. Scotus and Nox produced Aether and Dies (The Day). Hyginus and Cicero also suggest that they produced Eros, but Hesiod states that Eros emerged fully formed at creation. Scotus and Nox also fathered a large number of spirits or personifications:

- Amicitia (Philotes) • Amor (Eros) • Continentia (Sophrosyne) • Discordia (Eris) • Dolus (Dolos) • Epaphos • Epiphron • Euphrosyne • Fatum (Moros) • Fraus (Apate) • Invidentia (Nemesis) • Labor (Ponos) • Letum (Ker) • Metus (Deimos) • Miseria (Oizys) • Misericordia (Eleos) • Mors (Thanatos) • The Parcae (The Moirai) • Petulantia (Hybris) • Porphyrion • Querella (Momos) • Senectus (Geras) • The Somnia (The Oneiroi) • Somnus (Hypnos) • Styx • The Tenebrae (The Keres) • The Hesperides

Scotus is named as one of the *Dii Inferi* (the gods below), the shadowy collective of ancient Roman deities associated with death and the Underworld.

Sol (The Sun)

Roman Name(s): Sol, Sol Indiges, Sol Invictus
Greek Name(s): Ἥλιος, Hêlios, Helius, Helios
Etruscan Name(s): Usil

Sol is the god of the sun. He is the brother of Aurora (The Dawn) and Luna (The Moon).

Due to his position above the earth, Sol is believed to be an all-seeing witness who is invoked to oversee sworn oaths.

He is commonly depicted in art wearing a radiant crown and riding a quadriga (a chariot drawn by four horses, sometimes winged horses).

At the eastern edge of the world, Sol lives in a golden palace in Oceanus, the river that encircles the earth, personified by the god Oceanus.

Each morning his sister Aurora (The Dawn) announces his arrival and he travels across the sky to the west.

Some sources say that Aurora accompanies him on his entire journey.

At the end of the day when he reaches the land of the Hesperides (the evening nymphs) in the west, he then descends into a golden cup which takes him through the northern streams of Oceanus back to his home and rising place in the east.

According to one myth, Sol gave permission for his mortal son Phaethon to drive his chariot across the sky for one day. Despite many warnings of the seriousness of the task and the possible dangers, Phaethon's journey is disastrous as he cannot control the horses.

Jupiter struck Phaethon with a lightning bolt to stop him from riding too close to the earth and burning it or riding too far away from the earth and freezing it beyond salvation.

This is a cautionary tale of unheeded warnings and their consequences, which are often outside of the control of those who warn of them.

Sol is one of the *Dii Selecti* (the chosen gods), a list of the twenty principal gods of Roman religion according to author Varro (recorded by Augustine of Hippo in his work De Civitate Dei or The City of God in the 5th century CE).

According to Varro, who was of Sabine origin, Sol was originally worshipped by the Sabines in the Central *Apennine* Mountains before being adopted by the Romans.

The Somnia (The Dream Spirits)

Roman Name(s): Somnia
Greek Name(s): *Ονειρος*, *Ονειροι*, Oneiros, Oneiroi

The Somnia (dreams) are the thousand dark winged dream spirits. They are also referred to as the Tribe of Dreams.

The Somnia emerge each night from their home in the midst of Scotus (The Darkness) where the dark mists encircle the world and fill the deep hollows of the earth.

In Hesiod's Theogony, the Somnia (Oneroi) are the offspring of Nox (Nyx, The Night) with no father, whereas Hyginus and Cicero name Scotus (Erebus, The Darkness) as their father.

In the ancient world, dreams were not something that a person simply dreamed from their own mind (as in I *had* a dream), but rather, they were something external that was shown *to* them (as in I *saw* a dream, or a dream was *shown to* me).

Ovid in his Metamorphoses goes further and names Somnus (Sleep) as the father of the Somnia, and Pasithea (the personification of relaxation, meditation, and hallucinations) as their mother.

Ovid also names Morpheus (The Shaper of Dreams) as the leader of the Somnia. Morpheus appears in human form, Icelos or Phobetor appear as beasts, and Phantasos appears as inanimate objects.

Somnus (Sleep)

Roman Name(s): Somnus
Greek Name(s): Ὕπνος, Hypnos, Hypnus

Somnus is the personification of sleep. In some sources he is the fatherless son of Nox (The Night), while other sources state that his father is Scotus (Erebus, The Darkness).

Next to his twin brother Mors (Peaceful Death), Somnus lives in a cave in the Underworld where day and night meet, but where no sunlight or sound enters. His bed is made of ebony, and at the entrance to his cave there are poppies growing, along with other sleep inducing plants.

Somnus and Mors are the subject of a painting by John William Waterhouse called Sleep and His Half-Brother Death, depicting the two figures side by side. The lighter figure in the foreground is Sleep (Somnus) holding poppies in his hands, and the darker figure in the background is Death (Mors).

Somnus, and other descendents of Nox such as Mors and Morpheus, have long been metaphorically associated with trance, sleep, and death, and in art they have long been depicted with poppies, scattering poppies, or with poppies nearby.

With the revival of classical learning, this iconography continued in paintings from the Renaissance period onwards. The Pre-Raphaelite influenced painting Night and Sleep by Evelyn de Morgan in 1878 features Nox and Somnus figuratively travelling across the sky from east to west (left to right), scattering poppies as they go.

Somnus's wife is Pasithea, one of the youngest of the Charites who was promised to him by Juno, the Queen of the Gods in return for him causing Jupiter to fall asleep, affecting the course of the Trojan War in Juno's favour.

Pasithea's name has been translated by breaking it down into two elements *pasis* = acquired + *thea* = sight or vision. With the name meaning acquired sight, it has been interpreted that she is a source of hallucinations or visions, along with rest and relaxation.

Somnus and Pasithea produced the Somnia, the thousand dream spirits, of whom Morpheus (The Shaper of Dreams) is their leader. The Greeks knew the Somnia as the Oneiroi, who appear in dreams mimicking many forms. Morpheus appears in human form, Icelos or Phobetor appear as beasts, and Phantasos appears as inanimate objects.

Spes (Hope)

Roman Name(s): Spes
Greek Name(s): Elpis

Spes is the goddess, spirit, and personification of hope. She was worshipped as a state cult, and also in private devotions. She is usually depicted as a young woman, carrying flowers, or a cornucopia (a horn of plenty) in her hands. Some sources suggest that Spes is the mother of Fama, the goddess of fame, renown, and rumour.

Her Greek equivalent was Elpis, who did not have a formal cult in ancient Greece, as the Greeks were more sceptical about the concept of hope, sometimes believing it to be delusional, and finding no place for it in the philosophy of the Stoics and the Epicureans.

A temple dedicated to Spes (hope) and Fides (faith) was built outside the Carmental Gate to the city of Rome during the first of the Punic Wars (264 BCE to 241 BCE). It was restored in 213 BCE, and then again in 7 CE.

Spes became increasingly worshipped as a symbol of Imperial Hope, alongside Fides (faith), and Fortuna (fortune, luck) as divine personifications of virtues that were essential to the success of the Roman Empire.

To the Romans, these virtues came directly from the gods, rather than as divine powers that existed within the individual such as Fides (faith, fidelity, and trustworthiness), Virtus (virtue), and Mens (intelligence).

Summamus (Nocturnal Thunder)

Roman Name(s): Summanus

Summamus is the god of nocturnal thunder, distinct from Jupiter who is the god of diurnal (daylight) thunder. Perhaps this sharing of thunder by day and night is indicative of Summamus having been adopted into the Roman gods from the Etruscan or the Sabine traditions in around the 3rd century BCE. The origin and nature of Summamus were unknown to Ovid in 8 CE, who in his work Fasti (6, 731) mentions the temple of Summamus, but admits that he does not know who he is. Pliny the Elder believed that Sumamus was of Etruscan origin, as one of nine gods of thunder:

> *"Tuscorum litterae novem deos emittere fulmina existimant, eaque esse undecim generum; Iovem enim trina iaculari. Romani duo tantum ex iis servavere, diurna attribuentes Iovi, nocturna Summano, rariora sane eadem de causa frigidioris caeli)."*

> "Tuscan literature supposes nine gods to shoot lightning, and that they are of eleven kinds; from Jupiter is shot three kinds. The Romans keep only two of them, attributing the day to Jupiter, the night to Summanus, and of course the rarer ones because of the colder climate."

> Pliny the Elder, Naturalis Historia 2.53

According to Varro, who was of Sabine origin, Summamus was originally worshipped by the Sabines in the Central *Apennine* Mountains before being adopted by the Romans.

Summamus *is named as one of the Dii Inferi* (the gods below), the shadowy collective of ancient Roman deities associated with death and the Underworld.

The Tenebrae (The Spirits of Death)

Roman Name(s): Tenebrae, Leta
Greek Name(s): *Κηρ*, *Κηρες*, Kêr, Kêres, Keres

The Tenebrae are the female spirits of violent or cruel death, either on the battlefield, by accident, by murder, or by ravaging disease.

They are depicted as women with fangs and talons wearing bloody garments. They are the agents of the Parcae (The Fates, who measure out the life thread of every person) and Fatum (Doom, who drives people toward their inevitable destruction).

The Tenebrae are cravers of blood, and fight amongst each other to feast upon the dying, tearing the souls free from the mortally wounded bodies, sending them on their way to the Underworld.

The gods are sometimes described standing by their favourites on the battlefield beating the Tenebrae away from them.

They are the daughters of Nox (The Night) with no father. Other sources add Scotus (The Darkness) as their father. They were also known as the *Leta* (the deaths).

Dating back to the 5th century CE, vases depicting the Tenebrae were believed to have been part of apotropaic rites and rituals to ward off evil and keep the Tenebrae away.

The word apotropaic comes from the ancient Greek *apotrópaios* (ἀποτρόπαιος), from *apó* (ἀπό) = away + *trópos* (τρόπος) = turn), to turn things away, as in turning away evil.

Terra Mater, Tellus Mater (Mother Earth)

Roman Name(s): Tellus, Tellus Mater, Terra, Terra Mater
Greek Name(s): Γαια, Γαιη, Γη, Gaia, Gaiê, Gê, Gaea
Etruscan Name(s): Cel

Terra Mater or Tellus Mater is the personification of the earth. Her Greek counterpart is Gaia.

She is depicted as a voluptuous woman rising out of the earth or reclining in the earth, with a cornucopia (a horn of plenty), bunches of flowers, or fruit.

She was often worshipped side by side with Ceres (the goddess of agriculture) in rituals to the earth and fertility, during which both goddesses are referred to as the mothers of produce.

She was originally known as Tellus Mater (*Tellus* = the land + *Mater* = mother), particularly during the period of the Roman Republic (509 BCE to 27 BCE).

In the following period when Rome became an empire, the name Terra Mater (*Terra* = earth + *Mater* = mother) appeared and gradually became interchangeable or indistinguishable with the name Tellus Mater.

In the 4th century, Servius the Grammarian attempted to explain the difference between these two names by arguing that Terra is the *elementum* (element) of earth, as in the four classical elements: earth (*terra*), air (*ventus*), water (*aqua*), and fire (*ignis*). Tellus on the other hand is the functional sphere of the earth, the guardian deity of the earth and the globe itself.

Tellus Mater appears on the eastern side of the Ara Pacis (the altar of peace). The altar was commissioned by the Roman Senate in 13 BCE and consecrated in 9 BCE to honour the return of Augustus to Rome after three years in Hispania and Gaul.

Tellus Mater is one of the *Dii Selecti* (the chosen gods), a list of the twenty principal gods of Roman religion according to Varro (recorded by Augustine of Hippo in his work De Civitate Dei or The City of God in the 5th century CE).

Terra Mater appears in the Roman mosaic at Sentium (modern-day Sassoferrato, central-eastern Italy) which has been dated to around 200-250 CE. She is shown reclining in the foreground with representations of the four seasons around her, with Aion appearing in the background holding a wheel containing the signs of the zodiac representing the cycle of time.

Trivia (Magic, Spells, the Moon, and Crossroads)

Roman Name(s): Trivia
Greek Name(s): Ἑκατη, Ἑκατα, Hekatê, Hekata, Hecate, Hecata

Trivia (three ways) is the goddess of magic, spells, the moon, the night, crossroads, and ghosts.

She is the daughter of Perses (Destruction) and Asteria (The Starry One). Her Greek equivalent is Hecate.

She is often depicted holding a pair of torches, a key, snakes, or accompanied by dogs.

She later became depicted as three-formed or triple-headed.

In magical traditions, she is referred to as The Triple Goddess.

She was traditionally worshipped as a protector of the household along with Jupiter, Vesta, Mercury, and Apollo.

She also took on the role of a mother of angels, and mother and saviour of the Cosmic World Soul (Anima Mundi = the soul of the world).

Trivia's associations with three-way crossroads, the night time, and the moon, are combined in the astrological symbols which represent her.

Perhaps the most well-known of these astrological symbols is the triple-moon, a conjunction of three phases of the moon side by side: a waxing moon, a full moon, and a waning moon.

These three stages of the moon were equated to three stages of womanhood: maiden, mother, and crone (old woman).

Trivia's association with borders, city walls, doorways, and crossroads expanded to include the realms outside or beyond the world of the living, and also the transitions between those worlds.

She has the power to protect from spirits, but she can also decide not to intervene, or actively drive the spirits towards unfortunate individuals who are to be punished.

Trivia is named as one of the *Dii Inferi* (the gods below), the shadowy collective of ancient Roman deities associated with death and the Underworld.

Vejovis (Health, Healing, and Medicine)

Roman Name(s): Vejovis, Vejove, Veive, Vedius, Vediovis, Vediove, Aesculapius
Greek Name(s): Ἀσκληπιός, Asklēpiós, Asclepius
Etruscan Name(s): Veiove

Vejovis is the god of healing. He ultimately became strongly associated with the Greek god Asclepius, but his origins however are very different, and some might say shrouded in mystery.

He is depicted as a young man holding a bunch of arrows, lightning bolts, or a pilum (javelin) in his hand (iconography traditionally associated with a god of war and battle rather than a healer), and sometimes accompanied by a she-goat.

Vejovis was associated with volcanic eruptions, but his original role and function is unknown. He is occasionally identified with Apollo on account of his arrows, and a young version of Jupiter on account of his lightning bolts.

He is believed to be of Etruscan origin, but According to Varro, who was of Sabine origin, Vejovis was originally worshipped by the Sabines in the Central Apennine Mountains before being adopted by the Romans.

The varied spellings of the name Vejovis above suggest that his name was known, heard, and variously transliterated by several different Italic peoples (including the Etruscans and the Sabines) across the Italian peninsula, possibly pre-dating the foundation of Rome.

The Romans believed that he was one of the first gods to be born, and he was mostly worshipped in Rome and Bovillae in Latium. Temples were built in his honour on the Capitoline Hill and on the Tiber Island. The temple between the two peaks of the Capitoline Hill contained a statue of Vejovis carrying a bundle of arrows with a statue of a she-goat by his side.

Aulus Gellius in book V chapter XII of his *Noctes Atticae* (Attic Nights) written around 177 CE, speculated that Vejovis was a kind of dark opposite or counterpart of Jove (Jupiter). Perhaps this opposite aspect of Jupiter can be compared to that of the god Summamus who was associated with nocturnal thunder, whereas Jupiter was associated with thunder during the day. Gellius also states that the initial part of the name Ve- acts as a negative prefix in words like vesanus (insane) as the opposite of sanus (sane). Therefore Ve-Jovis is interpreted as anti-Jove (anti-Jupiter).

One possible connection with healing or the protection from illness and disease is that in spring time goats were sacrificed to Vejovis in order to avert plagues. According to Cicero, Vejovis had three festivals in the Roman Calendar on the 1st January, 7th March, and 21st May.

Vejovis is named as one of the *Dii Inferi* (the gods below), the shadowy collective of ancient Roman deities associated with death and the Underworld.

The Roman Gods   An Illustrated Introduction

The Venti (The Winds)

84

Roman Name(s): Venti
Greek Name(s): Ἄνεμοι, Ánemoi, Anemoi

The Venti are the personifications of the winds based on where they come from, their points of origin on the compass, and the seasons they represent. The first four to be named were Aquilo (the North Wind), Vulturnus (the East or Southeast Wind), Auster (the South Wind), and Favonius (the West Wind).

The Tower of Winds in Athens, built around the first century BCE, is the only surviving horologium (clock tower) that remains from classical antiquity. On each of its eight sides is a relief sculpture of the winds as follows:

	NW	N	NE
Roman Name(s)	Caurus, Corus	Aquilo, Septentrio	Caecius
Greek Name(s)	Skiron (Σκίρων)	Boreas (Βορέας)	Kaikias (Καϊκιάς)
	W		**E**
Roman Name(s)	Favonius		Subsolanus
Greek Name(s)	Zephyrus (Ζέφυρος)		Apeliotes (Απελιώτες)
	SW	**S**	**SE**
Roman Name(s)	Africus	Auster	Vulturnus
Greek Name(s)	Libs (Λιψ)	Notos (Νότος)	Eurus (Εὖρος)

While the main four winds were the first to be named and remained fairly static, additional lesser winds were added, and some of their names changed over time.

Claudius Ptolemy (c. 100 - c. 170 CE) was an Alexandrian mathematician, astronomer, astrologer, geographer, and music theorist. His work Geography or Geographical Guidance is the basis for Ptolemy's World Map which is believed to have been produced by Agathodaemon of Alexandria in around the second century CE, based on the details given in Ptolemy's book.

In this map the winds are illustrated and named around the edges of the map, but instead of four (one every 90 degrees), or eight (one every 45 degrees), there are twelve of them (one every 30 degrees) which are as follows (clockwise from North):

• Septentrio or Aparctias • Aquilo or Boreas • Cecias or Apeliotes • Subsolanus • Vulturnus or Eurus • Euronotus • Auster or Notus • Libonotus or Euroauster • Africus or Libs • Favonius or Zephyrus • Caurus / Chorus or Iapix Sive Argestes • Circrus or Tresiias).

The Ptolemy map was the basis for the 1467 map of the world by Nicolaus Germanus. The Venti were included in several world maps up until the 16th century, such as those of Martin Waldseemuller (1507), Lorenz Fries (1522), Battista Agnese (1544), Giacomo Gastaldi (1548), Sebastian Munster (1550), and Abraham Ortelius (1564).

The Venti are agreed upon by many sources to have been born of Astraeus (The Dusk), and Aurora (The Dawn). Astraeus was associated with the winds because of his sons, and also because it was believed that the winds were most active at dusk.

Venus (Love, Lust, Passion, and Procreation)

Roman Name(s): Venus
Greek Name(s): *Αφροδιτη*, *Aphroditê*, Aphrodite
Etruscan Name(s): Turan, Apru

Venus is the goddess of love, divine beauty, lust, pleasure, passion, and procreation. She is often depicted as divinely beautiful, representing an idealised form of femininity, and often accompanied with iconic symbols such as seashells, myrtles, roses, doves, sparrows, and swans. The Astrological symbols for Venus and her Greek equivalent Aphrodite are believed to represent a copper hand mirror with a handle, or a necklace with a pendant. In the 1750s the Swedish biologist Carl Linnaeus introduced the convention of using this symbol to represent the female sex.

As well as being the equivalent of the Greek goddess Aphrodite, she is also similar to the Phoenician goddess Astarte, the Mesopotamian goddess Ishtar, the Etruscan goddess Turan (Apru), the Egyptian goddess Hathor or Isis, and even the Norse goddess Freyja. Venus originally represented fertility and springtime, but from around the third century BCE, additional iconography in common with the Greek Aphrodite was adopted.

She is the mother of the Trojan hero Aeneas in Greek mythology, and Roman tradition claimed Aeneas as the founder of Rome. Venus then became venerated as Venus Genetrix, the mother of the entire Roman nation. Roman emperors claimed to be ultimately descended from her, and she took on the role of divine guardian.

Venus is one of the *Dii Selecti* (the chosen gods), a list of the twenty principal gods of Roman religion according to Varro (recorded by Augustine of Hippo in his work De Civitate Dei or The City of God in the 5th century CE).

Veritas (Truth)

Roman Name(s): Veritas
Greek Name(s): Ἀλήθεια, Aletheia

Veritas is the goddess and personification of truth and truthfulness. She was considered important as one of the main virtues that any good Roman should posess, often depicted as a virgin dressed in white and holding a hand mirror.

Some sources state that Veritas is the daughter of Saturn, while some say that Jupiter is her father, and others suggest that Veritas is the creation of Prometheus.

Veritas is also the mother of Virtus, the goddess of bravery and virtue, particularly on the battlefield.

The Greek equivalent of Veritas is believed to be Aletheia, although this is debated with regard to the Greek and Roman concepts of truth that these goddesses embody and represent.

The Greek goddess Aletheia represents truth as unconcealment, disclosure, nothing hidden, the truth being visible. The Roman goddess Veritas also represents truth as an understanding of rightness and justice.

The name Veritas representing the virtue of truth and truthfulness has been adopted into many Latin mottos of many colleges, universities, and other organisations.

Vertumnus (The Change of Seasons)

Roman Name(s): Vertumnus, Vortumnus, Vertimnus
Etruscan Name(s): Voltumna

Vertumnus is the god of seasons, the change of seasons, plant growth, gardens, and fruit trees. The name *Vortumnus* most likely derives from the Etruscan *Voltumna*, influenced by the Latin verb *vertere* meaning to change, i.e. the changing of the seasons.

Varro was convinced that Vortumnus was a major god in the Etruscan pantheon. The cult of Vertumnus arrived in Rome around 300 BCE, and a temple in his honour was constructed on the Aventine Hill by 264 BCE.

Vertumnus also has the power to change his form at will, according to Ovid in his Metamorphosis (xiv), Vertumnus disguised himself as an old woman in order to gain entry into the orchard of the goddess Pomona. In his disguise, he proceeded to tell Pomona the story of Iphis and Anaxarete, a cautionary tale about the dangers of rejecting a suitor and being turned into stone, as a pre-text to seducing her. Vertumnus and Pomona were both celebrated in the festival of Vertumnalia on the 13th day of August.

The tale of Vertumnus and Pomona is considered perhaps the first uniquely Latin tale. It inspired artists of the Renaissance and Baroque periods, sculptors, painters, etc. to depict scenes or allegories inspired by the tale, such as Giuseppe Arcimboldo (c1590), Luca Giordano (c1682-1683), Francesco Penso (1717), and Jean-Baptiste Lemoyne (1760).

Vesta (The Sacred Fire)

Roman Name(s): Vesta
Greek Name(s): Ἑστια, Hestia, Hestia

Vesta is the goddess of the hearth, the fireplace, the symbolic focal point of the home, and by extension, the home in general, domesticity, and community. The astrological symbols for Vesta and her Greek equivalent Hestia represent a hearthstone, a fire, or a flame.

She was devoured by her father Saturn as an infant due to Saturn's fear of being overthrown by his offspring. With assistance, Vesta's youngest brother Jupiter forced Saturn to vomit them all back up from his stomach. Vesta was a very important goddess in ancient Rome, with public hearths serving as a focal point for towns and cities.

As the goddess of sacred and sacrificial fire, Vesta received the first offering in every household, and the first and last libations of wine. Founders of city states or colonies would ask for permission from their mother city, and whenever a new colony was established, a flame from Vesta's public hearth would be carried to the new settlement.

Vesta is traditionally depicted simply wearing a cloak and a head veil, sometimes with a staff in her hand, next to a fire. Her throne is plain and wooden, with a white woollen cushion.

The priestesses of Vesta, known as Vestal Virgins, administered the temple and kept the flame burning. As the keeper of the flame at Olympus, Vesta is considered to be the first Vestal Virgin. Vesta is one of the *Dii Selecti* (the chosen gods), a list of the twenty principal gods of Roman religion according to Varro (recorded by Augustine of Hippo in his work De Civitate Dei or The City of God in the 5th century CE).

Victoria (Victory)

Roman Name(s): Victoria
Greek Name(s): *Νικη*, Nikê, Nike
Etruscan Name(s): Meanpe

Victoria is the goddess and personification of victory, both on the battlefield in times of war, and in any form of competition, athletic or otherwise, in times of peace. Her Greek equivalent is Nike.

The Romans became aware of Nike during the first Punic War, as a goddess of their Greek allies. She was worshipped in Magna Graecia, the Greek speaking coastal areas of Southern Italy and in mainland Greece.

At around the same time, Roman war deities began to receive the epithet victor (conqueror), or invictus (unconquered). By the time the Roman Republic transitioned into the Roman Empire, Victoria had become popular with the Roman military and the civilian population, in association with other deities, and in her own right. She is most commonly depicted with wings, wearing golden sandals, in flight or leaning forward holding a crown of victory in the form of a laurel wreath or a palm frond.

Victoria is sometimes described as an attribute of Minerva with some statues depicting her standing in the palm of Minerva's hand. She was widely invoked during the Punic Wars against Ancient Carthage, and she had her own temple on the Palatine Hill, the central and most ancient of the Seven Hills of Rome.

Rome's eventual victory over Carthage was seen as Victoria's blessing, and confirmation of Rome's divinely given right to rule over other states.

Virtus (Bravery and Virtue)

Roman Name(s): Virtus
Greek Name(s): *Αρετη*, Arete

Virtus is the goddess of bravery and virtue. She is closely associated with Honos, the god of honour. Thus, honour and virtue were important ideals for the Romans, particularly valour and bravery on the battlefield. Her Greek equivalent is Arete, whose name also means excellence of any kind, i.e. a person's full realisation of their potential.

During the Second Punic War, Roman General and politician Marcus Claudius Marcellus restored the temple of Honos, and built a second adjoining shrine to Virtus, making it a double-temple, finally dedicated after his death by his son in 205 BCE.

The design of the double-temple was such that one had to enter the temple of Virtus before the temple of Honos, symbolising that honour cannot be reached without virtue, i.e. military success.

The Virtus and Honos double-temple was again restored by Vespasian, who ruled from 69 to 79 CE, after which it remained standing well into the fourth century CE.

Another temple to Virtus and Honus was built by Gaius Marius after the Roman victory in the Cimbrian war in 101 BCE. It was built using the spoils captured from the defeated Cimbri and the Teutones.

Virtus appears in the story of Hercules, where Hercules finds himself at a crossroads, where he has to choose between Virtus and Voluptas (i.e. virtue and vice). One road leads to a life of ease and gluttony, and the other leads to a life of valour and strength. Hercules eventually chooses Virtus.

Volturnus (The Rivers)

Roman Name(s): Volturnus, Tiberinus

For the Romans, the river Tiber was the most significant of rivers, as the city of Rome was founded on its eastern banks. As legend has it, the founders of Rome, twin brothers Romulus and Remus were abandoned and exposed on the banks of the Tiber, until they were rescued and suckled by a she-wolf.

In the Greek and Roman traditions, rivers and other bodies of water had spirits, personifications, gods, and goddesses attributed to them.

The Romans worshipped Tiberinus, the god of the river Tiber. Obscure rituals were held where offerings were placed into the Tiber during the month of May, including straw figures which were collected from 27 stations around the city in procession.

Volturnus was originally an Etruscan god of all rivers, and when his worship spread to Rome, he appears to have been combined with Tiberinus, perhaps interpreted as the same god with different names, or as the same god with an aspect or epithet associated and named with the river Tiber (e.g. *Volturnus Tiberinus*).

A festival in honour of Volturnus called Volturnalia was celebrated on the 27th day of August.

Volturnus is one of the minor *Dii Flaminales*, gods who were cultivated by flamines, special priests who were assigned to the official cults during the Roman Republic. By the late Roman Republic however he appears to have vanished into obscurity.

Vulcan (Blacksmith of the Gods)

Roman Name(s): Vulcanus, Vulcan
Greek Name(s): Ἡφαιστος, Hêphaistos, Hephaestus
Etruscan Name(s): Sethlans

Vulcan is the god of fire, smithery, craftsmen, metallurgy, metalworking, stonemasonry, and sculpture.

He is often depicted as a bearded man holding tools of smithery such as a hammer or a pair of tongs.

Vulcan is a master-crafter capable of creating objects with special properties.

He serves as blacksmith to the gods and makes all of their equipment, thrones, and weapons.

Vulcan designed Hermes's winged helmet and sandals, Aphrodite's girdle, Helios's chariot, and Eros's bow.

In later accounts he worked with the help of the Cyclopes, among them Brontes (Thunder), Stereops (Lightning), and Arges (Flash), who famously designed Jupiter's thunderbolt.

According to Homer's Iliad, Vulcan built a number of automatons made of metal to work for him or for others. This included tripods with golden wheels, able to move at his wish in and out of the assembly of the hall of the celestials:

Vulcan is the son of Juno, and although it is not certain that Jupiter is his father, Jupiter is described in such a way. In one account Juno rejected Vulcan and threw him from the heavens because of his physical impairment at birth. Vulcan fell into the ocean and was cared for and raised by Thetis and Eurynome.

Another account suggests that Jupiter threw Vulcan out of the heavens for obstructing his advances towards Juno. Vulcan fell for a whole day and landed on the island of Lemnos, where he was taught to be a master craftsman by the Sintians, an ancient tribe native to the area, and Vulcan's physical disability was due to the fall.

Vulcan is one of the *Dii Selecti* (the chosen gods), a list of the twenty principal gods of Roman religion according to Varro (recorded by Augustine of Hippo in his work De Civitate Dei or The City of God in the 5th century CE).

Vulcan is one of the minor *Dii Flaminales*, gods who were cultivated by flamines, special priests who were assigned to the official cults during the Roman Republic.

According to Varro, who was of Sabine origin, Vulcan was originally worshipped by the Sabines in the Central *Apennine* Mountains before being adopted by the Romans.